THE WILD GEESE

OGAI MORI

THE
WILD
GEESE

translated by
KINGO OCHIAI
and
SANFORD GOLDSTEIN

CHARLES E. TUTTLE COMPANY
Rutland, Vermont & Tokyo, Japan

Representatives

For Continental Europe:
BOXERBOOKS, INC., Zurich

For the British Isles:
PRENTICE-HALL INTERNATIONAL, INC., London

For Australasia:
BOOK WISE (AUSTRALIA) PTY. LTD.
104-108 Sussex Street, Sydney 2000

Published by the
Charles E. Tuttle Co., Inc.
of Rutland, Vermont
and Tokyo, Japan
with editorial offices at
Suido 1-chome, 2-6, Bunkyo-ku, Tokyo

Library of Congress
Catalog Card No.
59-14087

International
Standard Book No.
0-8048-1070-2

First edition, 1959
Thirteenth printing, 1983

Printed in Japan

MORE THAN half a century ago the author of *The Wild Geese* recognized the difficulty of solving one of Japan's major problems, the adoption of Western values and the preservation of her own. He lived at a time when Japan was becoming increasingly aware of external influences; he was to reflect those influences in his career as a major figure in modern Japanese literature.

In 1870, the third year of Emperor Meiji's reign, the precocious Rintaro Mori (1862–1922), who was later to adopt the pen name Ogai Mori, was learning Dutch, a language regarded at that time as indispensable to a knowledge of Western medicine. The tutor was Ogai's father, a physician to a feudal lord. That study of language started Ogai on a lifelong interest in the West. His father took him to Tokyo in 1872 to learn German at a private school, and two years later the boy of twelve, recording his age as fourteen, entered the preparatory course of Tokyo Medical College, soon to become the Medical Faculty of Tokyo University. For a period of time at the end of his college career, Ogai lived in the Kamijo, the boardinghouse frequently mentioned in *The Wild Geese*.

Graduating at nineteen, Ogai assisted his father for several months in his practice and then decided to become an army surgeon. In 1884 the army sent Ogai to Germany to study military hygiene. During his four-year stay, successively at the Universities of Leipzig, Munich, and Berlin, he wrote and published several theses in German which undoubtedly strengthened his understanding of the scientific method and perhaps helped him form the basis for the logical structure of his later works of fiction.

His travels abroad had profound effects, for the year after Ogai's return to Japan in 1888, he translated and published an anthology of French and German poems, and at one time or another during his career he brought to Japan's literary public selections from Hans Christian Andersen, Goethe, Ibsen, Wilde, Shakespeare, and many other European novelists and dramatists. Except for an unsuccessful first marriage that ended in divorce, all seemed to be going well with Ogai. He established himself as an important writer, received an advanced degree in medicine, and earned promotions as Director of the Military Medical College and as Chief of the Medical Staff to the Imperial Guard Division.

Then, in 1899, Ogai was transferred to an army medical post in Kyushu. The change, a radical one in which his creative activity declined, made him think of his tour of duty as a period of exile. "The writer Ogai," he wrote, "died there." But the military man served without complaint. Perhaps the Kyushu period had its positive aspect in helping Ogai define "resignation," a key word in his vocabulary and one especially important in *The Wild Geese*. To Ogai, the word means serenity of mind which enables one to calmly observe the world and one's self. The three-year "exile" undoubtedly gave Ogai time for introspection, but a more active life awaited him when, in 1902, he returned to Tokyo to assume other duties and then, two years later, when he served at the front during the Russo-Japanese War. Yet he was shortly to figure as a leading writer standing against a growing tendency— one, ironically enough, that originated in Europe.

In the first decade of the twentieth century, often called the period of naturalism in modern Japanese literature, Zola and Maupassant were models for young Japanese writers who exploited the sordid both in society and in their own private lives. One might have expected Ogai to join the new school, but along with the gifted writer Soseki Natsume (1867–1916), Ogai objected to the subordinate role of reason, of intelligence, in the deterministic philosophy of the naturalists. Natsume stimulated Ogai to further creativity, and in 1909 Ogai began his own literary journal, *The Pleiades*. In three years, in addition to essays and translations, he wrote no fewer than thirty stories and plays, of which two major works, *Vita Sexualis* and *A Youth*, present markedly Ogai's criticism of naturalism.

Ogai's antagonism toward this new movement perhaps deepened his recognition of the richness of his own culture. Born into a samurai family, raised from early childhood in Confucian and feudal culture, Ogai, who began the study of Chinese classics at the age of four, had no particular reason to revolt against tradition. At an early age he had been given the opportunity to investigate the West. The new might have easily overwhelmed him. His return from abroad found him sensitively alert to the powerful influences of the West. His natural perspicacity, his linguistic proficiency, his serious intellectual pursuits in Germany—all these contributed to his understanding. Yet, unlike many of those who had been to Europe, he was not content to be simply a retailer of new knowledge. With new thoughts assimilated into the complex of his own personality, he tried to awaken and enlighten his backward country. He saw the chaos in Japan, the chaos of the old and new in collision everywhere, and he attempted, through science and literature, to give his country the harmony, the order, it needed.

Earlier he had written stories of contemporary life; in the last decade of his career he was to shift his focus to stories of the past. In 1912, on the funeral day of the great Emperor whose reign was characterized by the adoption of things Western, Ogai completed the first of his historical novels. He concentrated on little-known personalities, men and women who subordinated personal interest to some transcendent cause, one they obeyed humbly.

Gan or *The Wild Geese,* a long story first published in twelve issues (1911–1913) of *The Pleiades,* focuses on a usurer and his wife, a poor old man and his daughter, a student and a mistress. Duty seems to submerge the individual soul, symbolically represented by the un-restrained flock of birds. But not all wild geese can fly, and in Ogai's novel there are several that cannot.

For the Japanese concerned with the traditions of his own culture, *The Wild Geese* recaptures the earlier Tokyo, the old Edo in the beginning decades of Meiji. But even Western readers will appreciate the detailed route of Okada's walks, the environs of the old Tokyo University, the lonely slope called Muenzaka. Ogai records the activities of university students, their boardinghouse lives, their bookstore browsing, their moments of escape. Store-keepers, strolling performers, servants, geisha, policemen —Ogai gives his readers glimpses of these, genre paintings of nineteenth-century Japan, portraits past and even present.

For Ogai that external world is important; its psycho-logical counterpart is equally so. Ogai watches his main characters, orders their movements, records their prob-lems. His line of reasoning goes ahead, falls back, remains suspended in mid-air: what to say to one's daughter, when to repay an obligation, how to guard one's thought. This inner world struggles with the ques-tions of silence and communication, duty and freedom, restraint and compulsion. Ogai's vision is unmistakably Japanese; on the other hand, the problems of the ex-pected and unanticipated, of tradition and emancipation, of pattern and change, concern men everywhere.

The eyes of Ogai Mori are gifted ones. They observe,

sometimes with affection, sometimes with irony, but always accurately. And the main impression they leave behind is that of the writer's sensitive compassion for man. That no simple answers emerge in the narrative, that no problems are solved, that the story comes full circle on the wings of dilemma, that more is implied than stated, that the novel's "uneventfulness" is nevertheless part of a world of tension and conflict—these are major elements in the art with which Ogai Mori accomplished this mature work.

KINGO OCHIAI
Niigata University

SANFORD GOLDSTEIN
Purdue University

9

THE WILD GEESE

CHAPTER ONE

This story happened long ago, but by chance I remember that it occurred in 1880, the thirteenth year of Emperor Meiji's reign. That date comes back to me so precisely because at the time I lodged in the Kamijo, a boardinghouse which was just opposite the Iron Gate of Tokyo University, and because my room was right next to that of the hero of the story. When a fire broke out inside the house in the fourteenth year of Meiji, I was one of those who lost all of their possessions when the Kamijo burned to the ground. What I'm going to put down, I remember, took place just one year before that disaster.

Almost all the boarders in the Kamijo were medical students, except for the few patients who went to the hospital attached to the university. It's been my observation that a residence of this kind is controlled by one of its members, a lodger who rises to a position of authority because of his money and shrewdness. When he passes through the corridor before the landlady's room, he always makes it a point to speak to her as she sits by the square charcoal brazier. Sometimes he'll squat opposite her and exchange a few words of gossip. Sometimes he seems to think only of himself when he throws saké parties in his room and puts the landlady out by making her prepare special dishes, yet the truth is that he takes care to see that she gets something extra for her troubles. Usually this type of man wins respect and takes advantage of it by having his own way in the house.

The man in the room next to mine was also powerful in the Kamijo, but he was of a different breed.

This man, a student called Okada, was a year behind me, so he wasn't too far from graduating. In order to explain Okada's character, I must speak first of his striking appearance. What I really mean is that he was handsome. But not handsome in the sense of being pale and delicately thin and tall. He had a healthy color and a strong build. I have hardly ever come across a man with such a face. If you force me to make a comparison, he somewhat resembled the young Bizan Kawakami, whom I got to know later than the time of this story, and who became destitute and died in misery. Okada, a champion rower in those days, far surpassed the writer Bizan in physique.

A good-looking face may influence others, but it alone does not carry weight in a boardinghouse. Personal behavior must also be considered, and I doubt if many students lived as well-balanced a life as Okada did. He wasn't a bookworm who worked greedily for examination marks each term and who wanted to win a scholarship. Okada did the required amount of work and was never lower than the middle of his class. And in his free time he always relaxed. After supper he would take a walk and would return without fail before ten. On Sundays he rowed or set off on a long hike. Except for periods of living with his crew before a match or of returning to his home in the country for summer vacations, the time never varied when he was in or out of his room. Often a boarder who had forgotten to set his watch by the signal gun at noon went to Okada's room to find out the time. And occasionally even the office clock in the Kamijo was put right by Okada. The more we observed him, the stronger became our impression that he was reliable. Even though Okada didn't flatter the landlady or spend much money above his room and board, she began to praise him. Needless to say, the fact that he paid his rent regularly was one of the reasons for her attitude.

14

She often said: "Look at Mr. Okada!"

But, anticipating her words, some of the students would say: "Well, we can't all be like him."

Before anyone realized it, Okada had become a model tenant.

Okada had regular routes for his daily walks. He would go down the lonely slope called Muenzaka and travel north along Shinobazu Pond. Then he would stroll up the hill in Ueno Park. Next he went down to Hirokoji and, turning into Naka-cho—narrow, crowded, full of activity —he would go through the compound of Yushima Shrine and set out for the Kamijo after passing the gloomy Karatachi Temple. Sometimes he made a slight variation in a particular route, such as a right turn at the end of Naka-cho, so that he would come back to his room along the silence and loneliness of Muenzaka.

There was another route. He occasionally entered the university campus by the exit used by the patients of the hospital attached to the medical school because the Iron Gate was closed early. Going through the Red Gate, he would proceed along Hongo-dori until he came to a shop where people were standing and watching the antics of some men pounding millet. Then he would continue his walk by turning into the compound of Kanda Shrine. After crossing the Megane-bashi, which was still a novelty in those days, he would wander for a short while through a street with houses on only one side along the river. And on his way back he went into one of the narrow side streets on the western side of Onarimichi and then came up to the front of the Karatachi Temple. This was an alternate route. Okada seldom took any other.

On these trips Okada did little more than browse now and then in the secondhand bookstores. Today only two or three out of many still remain. On Onarimichi, the same shops, little changed from what they formerly were, continue to run their businesses. Yet almost all the stores on Hongo-dori have changed their locations and their proprietors. On these walks Okada hardly ever turned right after leaving the Red Gate because most of the streets narrowed so much that it was annoying. Besides, only one secondhand bookshop could then be found along that way.

Okada stopped in such shops because, to use a term now in vogue, he had literary tastes. In those days the novels and plays of the new school had not yet been published; as for the lyric, neither the haiku of Shiki nor the waka of Tekkan had been created. So everyone read such magazines as the *Kagetsu Shinshi*, which printed the first translation of a Western novel. In his student days Okada read with interest the happenings of the new era written in the style of classical Chinese literature. This was the extent of his literary tastes.

Since I've never been very affable, I didn't even speak to those students I met quite often on the campus except when I had a reason. As for the students in the boarding-house, I seldom tipped my cap in greeting. But I became somewhat friendly with Okada because of the bookshops. On my walks I wasn't as rigid in my direction as Okada was, but since I had strong legs, I let them direct me through Hongo to Shitaya and Kanda, and I paused in every secondhand bookstore. On such occasions I often met Okada inside.

I don't remember who spoke first, but I do recall the first words between us : " How often we meet among old books!"

This was the start of our friendship.

In those days at the corner down the slope in front of Kanda Shrine, we came across a shop which sold books on its stalls. Once I discovered the *Kimpeibai*, and I asked the storekeeper how much it was.

"Seven yen."

"I'll give you five," I said.

"A while back Okada offered six."

Since I had enough money with me, I gave the dealer what he asked.

But when I met Okada a few days later, he said: "You acted quite selfishly—you know I found the *Kimpeibai* first."

"The man at the shop said you bargained, but that you couldn't agree. If you must have it, buy it from me."

"Why should I? We're neighbors, so I can borrow it when you're through."

I agreed. *Both have literary tastes*

In this way, Okada and I, who had not until now been acquainted even though we lived at such close quarters, often began to call on each other.

CHAPTER TWO

EVEN IN the days I am writing about, the Iwasaki mansion was located, as it is today, on the southern side of Muenzaka, though it had not yet been fenced in with its present high wall of soil. At that time dirty stone walls had been put up, and ferns and horsetails grew among the moss-covered stones. Even now I don't know whether the land above the fence is flat or hilly, for I've never been inside the mansion. At any rate, in those days the copse grew thick and wild, and from the street we could see the roots of the trees, while the grass around them was seldom cut.

On the north side of the slope, small houses were constructed in clusters, and the best-looking among them had a clapboard fence. As for shops, there were only a kitchenware dealer's and a tobacconist's. Among the dwellings, the most attractive to the people who passed belonged to a sewing teacher, and during the day young women could be seen through the window going about their work. If the day was pleasant and the windows were open when we students passed, the girls, always talking, raised their faces and looked out into the street. And then once more they would continue their laughing and chattering.

Next to this house was a residence whose door was always wiped clean and whose granite walk I often saw sprinkled with water in the evening. During the cold weather the sliding doors were shut, but even during the hot weather the bamboo shutters were lowered. This house always seemed conspicuously quiet, the more so because of the noise in the neighboring one.

About September of the year of this story, Okada, soon after his return from his home in the country, went out after supper for his usual stroll, and as he walked down Muenzaka, he met by accident a woman on her way home from the public bath and saw her enter the lonely place next to the sewing teacher's. It was almost autumn, so people had less occasion to seek relief from the heat by sitting outside their houses, and the slope was now empty. The woman, who had just come to the entrance of that quiet house, was trying to open the door, but hearing the sound of Okada's clogs, stopped what she was doing and turned her face. The two stared at each other.

Okada was not very much attracted by the woman in kimono with her right hand on the door and her left hand holding her bamboo basket of toilet articles. But he did notice her hair freshly dressed in the ginkgo-leaf style with her sidelocks as thin as the wings of a cicada. He saw that her face was oval and somewhat lonely, her nose sharp, her forehead to her cheeks conveying an impression of flatness, though it was difficult to say exactly what made him think so. Since these were no more than momentary impressions, he had completely forgotten about her when he came to the bottom of the slope.

18

But about two days later he again took the same direction, and when he came near the house with the lattice door, he glanced at it, suddenly remembering the stranger from the public bath. He looked at the bow window with its vertically nailed bamboo canes and two thin, horizontal pieces of wood wound with vines. The window screen had been left open about a foot and revealed a potted plant. As he gave some attention to these details, he slowed down somewhat, and it took a few moments before he reached the front of the house.

Suddenly above the plant a white face appeared in the background where nothing but gray darkness had been. Furthermore, the face smiled at him.

From that time on, whenever Okada went out walking and passed this house, he seldom missed seeing the woman's face. Sometimes she broke into his imagination, and there she gradually started to take liberties. He began to wonder if she was waiting for him to pass or was simply looking outside with indifference and accidentally noticed him. He thought about the days before he had first come upon her, trying to recall if she had ever glanced out of the house or not, but all he could remember was that the house next to the noisy sewing teacher's was always swept clean and looked lonely. He told himself that he must have wondered about the kind of person who lived there, but he could not even be certain of that. It seemed to him that the screens were always shut or the bamboo blinds were drawn to reinforce the quiet behind them. He finally concluded that perhaps the woman had recently come to look outside and had opened the window to wait for his passing.

Each time he came by, they looked at each other, and all the while thinking about these events, Okada gradually felt he was on friendly terms with "the woman of the window." One evening, two weeks later, he unconsciously took off his cap and bowed when he passed her

19

house. Her faintly white face turned red, and her lonely smile changed into a beaming one.

From that moment on, Okada always bowed to the woman of the window when he went by.

CHAPTER THREE

OKADA's admiration of old Chinese romantic tales had caused him to take an interest in military sports, but since he had no opportunities for practicing them, this desire had never been satisfied. This might, however, explain his interest in rowing, which he had taken to a few years before. He had been so enthusiastic and had made so much progress that he became a champion rower. Obviously, this activity was a manifestation of his desire to practice martial arts.

A type of woman in these romantic tales also appealed to Okada. She is the woman who makes beauty her sole aim in life so that, with perfect ease, she goes through an elaborate toilet even while the angel of death waits outside her door. Okada felt that a woman should be only a beautiful object, something lovable, a being who keeps her beauty and loveliness no matter what situation she is in. Okada probably picked up this sentiment unconsciously, partly under the influence of his habitual reading of old Chinese romantic love poetry and the sentimental and fatalistic prose works of the so-called wits of the Ming and Ch'ing dynasties.

Even though a long interval had passed since Okada started bowing to the woman of the window, he would not investigate her personal history. From the appearance of the house and the way she dressed, he guessed that she might be someone's mistress. But this did not disturb him. He did not even know her name, and he made no effort to learn it. All he had to do was look at the name plate, but he couldn't bring himself to do this in her presence. At other times, when she wasn't there, he hesitated because of the neighbors and the passersby. As a result, he never looked at the characters written on the small wooden sign shadowed by the eaves.

CHAPTER FOUR

ALTHOUGH the events of this story that have Okada for their hero took place before I learned the earlier history of the woman of the window, it will be convenient to give an outline of that history here.

The narrative goes back to the days when the medical school of the university was located at Shitaya and the old guardhouse of Lord Todo's estate was turned into a student dormitory. Its windows, of vertical wooden bars as thick as a man's arms, were set at wide intervals in a wall of gray tiles plastered in checkerboard fashion. If I may phrase it this way, the students lived there like so many beasts, though I'm sorry to make such a comparison. Of course you can't see windows like those now except in the castle turrets of the emperor's palace, and even the bars of the lion and tiger cages in the Ueno Zoo are more slenderly made than those were.

The dormitory had servants whom the students could use for errands. They usually sent out to buy something cheap to eat, like baked beans or roasted sweet potatoes. For each trip the servant received two sen. One of these workers was called Suezo. The other men had loud mouths buried in bur-like beards, but this man kept his mouth shut and always shaved. The others wore dirty clothes of rough cotton; Suezo's were always neat, and sometimes he came to work wearing silk.

Suezo is unlike the other servants in appearance and most likely different in behavior also

21

I don't know who told me or when, but I heard that Suezo lent money to needy students. Of course it only amounted to fifty sen or one yen at a time. But when the debt gradually grew to five or ten yen, Suezo would make the borrower draw up a note, and if it wasn't yet paid at the end of the term, a new one was written. Suezo became what can really be called a professional moneylender. I haven't any idea how he obtained such capital. Certainly not from picking up two sen for each student errand. But perhaps nothing is impossible if a man concentrates all of his energies on what he wants.

At any rate, when the medical school moved from Shitaya to Hongo, Suezo no longer remained a servant, but his house, newly located on Ike-no-hata, was continually visited by a great number of indiscreet students. When he began working for the university, he was already over thirty, was poor, and had a wife and child to support. But since he had made quite a fortune through moneylending and had moved to his new house, he began to feel dissatisfied with his wife, who was ugly and quarrelsome.

At that time he remembered a certain woman he had seen every so often while he was still going to the university through a narrow alley from his house at the back of Neribei-cho. There was a dark house whose ditchboards in that alley were always partly broken and half of whose sliding shutters were closed all year round. At night, when anyone passed, he had to go sideways because of a wheeled stall drawn up under the eaves.

What first attracted Suezo's attention to this house was the music of the samisen inside. And then he learned that the person playing the instrument was a lovely girl about sixteen or seventeen years old. The neat kimono she wore was quite different from the shabby appearance of her house.

If the girl happened to be in the doorway, as soon as

22

she saw a man approaching she went back into the dark interior. Suezo, with his characteristic alertness, though without particularly investigating the matter, found out that the girl's name was Otama, that her mother was dead, and that she lived alone with her father, who sold sugary, sticky candies moulded into figures in his stall.

But eventually a change took place in this back-street house. The wheeled stall vanished from its set place under the eaves. And the house and its surroundings, which were always modest, seemed suddenly attacked by what was then fashionably called "civilization," for new boards over the ditch replaced the broken and warped ones, and a new lattice door had been installed at the entrance.

Once Suezo noticed a pair of Western shoes in the doorway. Soon after, a new name plate bearing a policeman's title was put up. Suezo also made certain, while shopping on the neighboring streets and yet without seeming to pry, that the old candy dealer had acquired a son-in-law.

To the old man, who loved his daughter more than sight itself, the loss of Otama to a policeman with terrifying looks was like having her carried off by a monster with a long nose and a red face. Otama's father had feared the discomfort he would incur by the intrusion of such a formidable son-in-law, and after meeting the suitor, had consulted with several confidants, but none of them had told him to reject the offer.

Someone said: "You see, I told you so, didn't I? When I took the trouble to arrange a good match, you were too particular, saying you couldn't part with your only child, so that finally a son-in-law you couldn't say no to is going to move in on you!"

And another said threateningly: "If you can't stand the man, the only other solution is to move far away, but since he's a policeman, he'll be able to catch up with you and make his offer again. There's no escaping him."

A wife who had a reputation for using her head was

believed to have told the old man: "Didn't I advise you to sell her off to a geisha house since her looks were good and her samisen master praised her skill? A policeman without a wife can go from door to door, and when he finds a pretty face, he takes her off whether you like it or not. You can't do anything but make the best of the bad luck that such a man took a fancy to your daughter."

No more than three months after Suezo had heard these rumors, he discovered one morning that the doors of the old candy dealer's house were locked and that an attached piece of paper gave notice that the house was for rent. Then, on inquiring further into the neighbors' talk while shopping, Suezo heard that the policeman had in his own native place a wife and children who had turned up on a surprise visit, whereupon a fight followed, and Otama ran from the house. A neighbor who overheard the quarrel stopped the girl from doing something rash. Not one of the old man's friends had enough knowledge about legal matters, so the old man had been quite indifferent about seeing if the marriage had been legally registered, and when the son-in-law told him he would completely handle the legal end of the marriage, the old man had had no suspicions or fears.

A girl at Kitazumi's grocery said to Suezo: "I really feel sorry for Taa-chan—she's honest and she had no doubt about the policeman, but he said he was only looking for a place to live."

And with his hand circling his cropped head of hair, the storekeeper interrupted her: "It's a pity about the old man too. He moved away because he couldn't stand meeting his neighbors and he couldn't stay here as before. But he still sells candy where he used to, saying he can't do business in places where there are no little customers. A while back he sold his stall, but now he has it again from the secondhand dealer, after telling him the situation. I think he's got financial troubles because of the

24

moving and such. It's as though the old man lived for only a short time in a world of dreams, freeing himself into easy retirement and keeping company with the policeman, who drank saké, acting like a god, while, in fact, he starved his wife and children in the country."

After that, the candy dealer's daughter slipped from Suezo's mind, but when he became financially well off and could do more of what he wanted, he happened to remember the girl.

Suezo, now with a wide circle of acquaintances to do his bidding, had them look for the old candy dealer and finally located his mean quarters next to a rickshaw garage behind a theatre. He learned also that the daughter wasn't married. So Suezo sent a woman to make overtures with an offer from a wealthy merchant disposed to have the girl for his mistress. In spite of Otama's objections at first, the old woman kept reminding the meek and reluctant girl of the advantages her father would get from the arrangement, and the negotiations reached the point where the parties agreed to meet at the Matsugen restaurant.

CHAPTER FIVE

BEFORE this new interest in Suezo's life, his only thoughts had centered on the students, their loans, and his returns, but he had no sooner located Otama and her father than he began to search his neighborhood for a house to establish his mistress in. He did not know whether or not he would succeed with his plan, but he was so eager to advance the scheme that he began to put it into operation. Two of the many houses he investigated pleased him. One of them was on his own street, halfway between his house, which was right next to the famous writer Fukuchi's, and the

25

Rengyokuan, which sold the best bowl of noodles in the area. A short distance from the Shinobazu pond was the house that had first appealed to him, for it stood somewhat back from the road, was fenced about with bamboo canes, and had a thick-needled parasol pine and a few cypresses.

The other house, in the middle of Muenzaka, was smaller. He did not find any notice on the door when he arrived, but he had heard that the house was for sale. Almost immediately upon entering, he discovered the noise from the neighboring house and the group of young ladies at work. "I don't like that," he said to himself, but on inspecting the interior with more care, he could not help appreciating the high quality of the timber. He knew that the former occupant, a wealthy merchant who had just died, had built the house with care in order to spend his retirement there. The place, with its front garden and granite doorway, was comfortable, neat, and superior in taste.

One night, as Suezo lay in bed, he thought about the two houses. His wife, who had tried to put her child to sleep, had herself dozed off while the infant suckled at her breast. Suezo turned away from her, her mouth open, snoring, the child pulling at the exposed breast.

Usually Suezo would lie awake in bed while devising new schemes for increasing the interest on his loans. His wife never complained about this habit, and she was usually asleep long before her husband.

Once more he glanced at her, thinking to himself: "Is that a woman's face? I doubt it. Take Otama's face. That's a woman's face, but I haven't seen her for a long time. You couldn't even call her a woman then. I wouldn't think she was more than a child. Yet even then—what a face! Gentle—yes. But with something smart in it too. It couldn't be worse now—better, I should think. How I'd love to see her now instead of that thing!"

Once more he looked down at the snoring woman.

"Poor devil!" he thought. "Sleeping there and not knowing a thing. She believes I'm adding up sums, but how wrong! How stupid and wrong! If you only knew—"

He suddenly slapped at his leg. "What! Mosquitoes out already! That's what's wrong with this section. Too many pests. We'll have to put up the net soon. Let the old she-devil get eaten alive, but I've got to think about the children."

His mind returned again to the question of the houses, and only after one o'clock in the morning had he made a decision. He had reasoned that he would prefer the Ike-no-hata place for its view, but what was the need of that when all he had to do was look out the window in the house he was now living in? One point in its favor was the cheap rent. That was true, but he remembered that a rented house has too many other expenses. Besides, it was not hidden enough. It would attract attention. What if one day he happened to leave the window open by mistake? He could just see the old devil on her way to market with the boy and girl. He could see them looking in and finding him there with Otama. There'd be more than that devil to pay!

When he thought about the Muenzaka house, he felt that it was somewhat gloomy, but the key point in its favor was its out-of-the-way location on a slope that only students seemed to stroll along at odd hours. But he didn't like the idea of putting up so much money for it. Still, with its timber. . . . And when he had it insured, he could at least get back what he paid at the beginning. "All right, then. That's it!" he told himself. "I'll take it. Take it and her."

Now he was especially pleased with it all. The future suddenly seemed real, and he saw himself on his evening of triumph. He had bathed carefully, had dressed smartly, had concocted an excuse to dodge his wife for the night. He saw himself rushing out of the house. He was free. He was almost to Muenzaka. He saw the light and wondered what it would be like when he went up the walk and opened the door. How radiantly beautiful her face would be! Poor Otama! There she was waiting for him, a kitten or some pet on her lap—ready to welcome him, of course—her face made-up, of course. He would dress her in a gorgeous kimono, would give her whatever she had demanded for the occasion. But he checked himself a moment. He wouldn't play the fool. He wouldn't spend his money unwisely. He had his connections at the pawn shops. How stupid to squander money like some men, like Fukuchi for example. Suezo suddenly saw his famous neighbor Fukuchi strutting openly on the streets and followed by his expensive geishas. The students would see the writer and be envious, but Suezo knew that the dandy was actually ill off. He was supposedly an intelligent man, a writer. But was he? If a clerk did the same kinds of nasty tricks with his pen as Fukuchi did, he would be discharged.

Suezo's thoughts returned to his Otama, and he suddenly remembered that she could play the samisen. Would she delight him with an intimate tune, plucking the strings with her fingers? No, it would be expecting too much of her, for she was young, inexperienced, only a policeman's temporary mistress. And he feared her shyness, feared she might say to him that evening: "I won't play. You'll only laugh at me." She might be shy in everything, in no matter what, and she might blush and fidget at the important moment.

Suezo's imagination shifted first one way and then another without restraint. The intensity increased until at last images shattered into fragments of flickering white skin and of whispered words tumbling into his ear.

With his wife still snoring beside him, he fell into a sweet sleep.

28

SUEZO thought of the approaching meeting with his future mistress at the Matsugen as a celebration.

We often hear that misers will even skin flints, but men who make large fortunes by thrift are not uniform in their behavior. Perhaps, as a group, these men give attention to such trifles as cutting sheets of toilet paper in half or filling out postcards with characters you cannot decipher without the aid of a microscope. Some of the most covetous are thrifty in every aspect of living, yet a few give themselves a breath of fresh air by leaving a loophole in their tight moneybags. Up to the present time the misers we have read about in novels or have seen on the stage seem to belong to the absolute type. But those we meet in life are not like that. Some of the most frugal loosen their purse strings to the final notch for women, and others gorge themselves with sumptuous foods.

I have already referred to Suezo's passion for clothing. Even during his difficult days of university employment, he was often completely transformed on holidays, his weekday outfit of inferior cotton replaced by a handsome kimono. He seemed like a smart-looking, successful merchant instead of a dormitory servant. This was a pleasure to him, and occasionally he dressed himself up in costly taffeta clothes and startled students who happened to pass and recognize him.

Dress had been Suezo's only hobby. He had not associated with geishas or prostitutes, and a night of saké at one of the drinking houses had been an impossibility. Even a bowl of noodles at the Rengyokuan had been a luxury for himself alone, and only recently had he permitted his wife and children to share the treat. He had not taken his wife out because he had not let her dress in a kimono to match his own expensive one. When she wanted a costly item for herself, he denied it to her.

"Don't talk like that," he had argued. "You and I are quite different. I've got to dress this way because of the men I associate with."

When Suezo's loans had started to bring in large sums, he began eating out. Yet he always justified the expense by going to a restaurant with his friends and never alone. But now that he was about to see Otama at the Matsugen, he wanted to make it a special affair, something gay and impressive. He had chosen the restaurant for that reason.

When the day of days drew near, Suezo wondered how he would dress Otama for the occasion. He would have spent any sum on her for the purpose, but since he had to provide for her father as well, he hesitated. The old go-between was at her wit's end for a solution, yet they both agreed that they had to consider the old man because any possible oversight might end their chances of getting Otama as a mistress.

The old man had told the go-between about his only child: "No," he had said, "I have no other relatives. And I've had a lonely time of it without my wife. She was over thirty when our first child was born. Our first and last. I kept Otama alive after her mother died in childbirth by taking her to different women in the neighborhood. They gave her their milk. And I had other troubles. When Otama was four, she had the measles during the Edo epidemic. The doctor said she'd die, but I didn't believe him. I took care of her. I saved her life. I let my business go, everything, watching over her. What a year! All sorts of terrible things happened two years after Lord Ii was killed. In that year some Westerners were beheaded at Namamugi. I couldn't even keep up my shop. More than once I was going to kill myself and Otama too. But how could I harm Otama? You should have seen her then. She had the smallest hands. How they poked at my chest! And she smiled at me with the widest eyes! We barely managed to live from one day to the next. I don't think many others could have gone through what we did. I wasn't a young man then. I was forty-five when she was born and, what with the cares I had, must have looked older. Still, I could have started over. One of my friends kept repeating the old proverb: 'When a single man can't live, two can.' Then he said he knew a widow who was looking for a husband. And he'd recommend me. Oh, she had money too! But I would have had to give my child away to someone else. How could I? I refused the offer flat."

Suddenly the old man paused, but a moment later he continued: "You don't know how I want to curse! You can't know what it is to feel that you've been tricked! Being poor made me a dull old man! I was there when that policeman made a plaything out of Otama. Yet she's not a bad girl, and they still speak of her as a fine daughter. You know, I'd like to marry her to a good man in the right way. That's the truth. But who to? No one's willing to take me along with her. I often said to myself: 'Don't give her away as a mistress! Don't!' But you say your master's a good man, an honest man, one we can trust? And a gentleman too? You see, I have to remember that Otama will be twenty next year. She has to marry soon. They say that the young shoot must be eaten before it withers. I'm trying to understand your offer. You see, I'm going to give away one so dear to me. You see, she's my only child. She's all I care about. I've got to meet this gentleman myself!"

When the go-between repeated these words to Suezo, he was disappointed at the old man's insistence that he be present at the interview. Suezo had planned to dismiss the go-between as soon as she had brought Otama to the restaurant. He expected no one to interfere. But if the father came, what a formal scene it would be! True, Suezo's mind bordered on formality, but it extended only to himself, as though he deserved recognition and praise

31

for bringing the meeting about and for taking the first step in satisfying his secret passion. For the event a tête-à-tête was essential. But the presence of a father would completely alter the tone of the holiday.

Previously the go-between had told him: "What a virtuous pair they are! At first they said no. They wouldn't even listen to me. But I got the girl alone and talked about duty, duty to her father. 'Your hard-working father,' I said. 'Too old to keep earning his living.' And that made her listen. She agreed to it all right. She got her father to agree!"

When Suezo learned this, his spirits soared, for he admired the tenderness and obedience of the person he was to own. Yet finding that both were pillars of purity, he felt that this important meeting would be like that of a bridegroom in front of his father-in-law. And the thought that the celebration might shift in that direction made him feel as though someone were pouring a dipper of ice water on his overheated head.

But he knew he had to be consistent, that he had to show his wealth and generosity. At last he agreed to give both father and daughter the necessary clothing. When he had further time to reason out his actions, he comforted himself, saying: "Since I'll have to take care of the father eventually when I get the daughter, I'm only doing in advance what I'll have to do later."

In such situations the customary procedure was to send the other party a definite sum of money to cover expenses. But Suezo had his own methods. He knew what was appropriate for the occasion, so he confided all the details to his tailor and ordered him to make adequate kimonos for the father and daughter. At the same time the go-between rushed off to ask Otama their measurements.

After the crone had left, Otama said to her father: "At least the man is considerate."

32

"Not sending the money shows he respects us," said the old man.

These were their reactions to Suezo's shrewd, penny-pinching methods.

CHAPTER SEVEN

SINCE fires seldom break out in the vicinity of Ueno Square and since the Matsugen hasn't burned down as far as I can remember, I think you can still find the room where the two parties met.

"I want something small and quiet," Suezo had said when he made the reservations, and on the appointed day he was led from the south entrance through a straight corridor that turned left into a room with an area of six mats.

When he was alone, he sat down on the cushion with his back to the alcove, which was adorned with an ukiyoe on a small scroll and a vase with a single twig of jasmine in it. He looked about with his usual care, examining everything.

Outside he saw a wooden fence that shut off the view of the pond. Perhaps he should have taken an upstairs room. But in an upstairs room they might have been seen from the street. Some years later the area around the pond was ruined and made into a race track, and then again, by one of those unusual transformations of the world, into a bicycle track. A long thin strip of land lying between the room and the fence was too narrow for a garden. From where he sat he could see a few pau-lownia trees, their trunks as smooth and glossy as if they had been polished with oiled rags. He also noticed a stone lantern and some small cypresses planted at intervals. In the busy street white clouds of dust rose, kicked up by the passersby, but here inside the enclosure the servants had sprinkled water over the moss to give the green an added freshness.

A maid came into the room carrying tea and an incense burner to drive away the mosquitoes. Placing the items before him, she asked: "And what dishes would you like served?"

"I'll tell you when my guests come," he said, dismissing her.

Once more alone, he took out his pipe. On entering, he had thought the room too warm, but after some time he put down the soiled fan the maid had given him, for occasional drafts of cool wind came through the corridors along with faint yet distinct odors from the kitchen and the toilets.

Leaning against the pillar of the alcove, Suezo watched the smoke drift. He thought of the earlier Otama, the pretty girl he had caught glimpses of as he passed her house. A pretty girl, yes, but really a child. What kind of woman had she changed into? What would she look like in her new kimono? A shame that the old man was coming with her! How long would he stay? Could he be sent home, removed somehow or other?

Suezo was startled out of his daydreaming by a samisen's being tuned in the room above him.

Then he heard the footsteps of two or three persons along the corridor.

" Your guests," said the maid, thrusting her face into the room.

"Come now! Step in! Let's not have any distance between you! Our master's open-minded!" said the go-between in a voice as noisy as a cricket's.

Suezo got to his feet and hurried out to the corridor. He saw the stooped figure of the old man as he hesitated near the corner wall and, behind him, Otama. She stood calmly, not at all overwhelmed, her eyes taking in everything with curiosity. The vision of a chubby girl with a pretty face swept through Suezo's mind, but the woman who appeared before him was totally different. Time had changed her. She was a thin, graceful beauty. She had arranged her hair in the style of a future bride and was without the customary makeup demanded on such occasions. Suezo had prepared himself for the pleasure, but he had not expected that the woman would be as she was. His eyes probed and registered. She was beyond anything he had imagined, and, for that, all the more beautiful.

Otama was also surprised. She had previously thought that she did not care what the merchant was like. She would sell herself to anyone, no matter what his personality. She would do anything for her father. But on seeing Suezo's dark features, his keen but engaging eyes, and his elegant yet restrained kimono, she felt momentarily relieved, like a person escaping from a hopeless situation.

"Please," said Suezo politely to the old man, "come in."

He spoke first to the old man and pointed to the interior of the room.

"Please," he repeated, turning to Otama.

After the father and daughter had entered the room, Suezo called the go-between to a sheltered part of the corridor, put some money wrapped in paper into her hand, and whispered into her ear. The woman smiled, her teeth stained with traces of black dye, and bowing her head several times in appreciation and laughing contemptuously, she hurried away along the corridor.

When Suezo returned, he found his guests huddled together at the entrance.

"Come now. Sit down. Please—on these cushions." This done, he called out: "And now for the dishes!"

Soon saké and some light refreshments were brought

in. As Suezo filled the old man's cup and exchanged a few words with him, he could tell from his manner that he had seen better days and had not simply dressed up for his first visit to a fancy restaurant.

At the beginning, Suezo had thought of the old man as a nuisance and was annoyed at having him there, but when he began to talk confidentially, Suezo's attitude softened. He went out of his way to make himself pleasant to the old man and to show the good he had in him. Inwardly Suezo was glad that he had been offered an opportunity to win Otama's trust by treating her father in this way.

By the time the dishes had been carried into the room, it seemed as though all three of them had dropped in to dine after a family excursion. Suezo, who was usually a tyrant in his own home and who was alternately obeyed and resisted by his wife, felt a placid and delicate delight that he had never felt before when he saw Otama take up a saké bottle and fill his cup, her face blushing and revealing a modest smile. While Suezo knew intuitively and unconsciously a happiness whose shadow floated like a vision in Otama's presence, he lacked the fine reasoning that would have made him reflect why his home life was devoid of such happiness, nor could he calculate how much was required to maintain such an unusual feeling —in fact, whether or not the requirement might be satisfied by him and his wife.

"Please!" shouted a voice against the beating of a pair of wooden clappers just outside the fence. "Your favorite actors!"

Upstairs the music stopped, and a maid said something from the railing.

"Thank you," said the man outside. And he called out the names of two Kabuki players.

The actor-imitator began to perform at once.

"We're lucky," said the maid, entering the room with

another container of saké. "A real mimic's come to-night!"

"What's that?" asked Suezo. "Are there false mimics along with the true ones?"

"Oh, yes. Lately, a university student's been going around."

"You mean he can actually play an instrument too?" asked Suezo.

"Of course, just like a professional. Even his costume's real. But we know him! We can tell who he is by his voice."

"Then there's only one deceiver," said Suezo.

"Yes, only one who dares!" said the maid, laughing.

"Do you know him personally?" Suezo asked.

"Why, yes! He often comes here to eat."

"He must have quite a skill then," said the old man. "And just think—he's only a student."

"But probably a bad one," said Suezo with an ironic smile as he thought of the students who came to his house. Some of them, he knew, disguised themselves as trades-men and teased the prostitutes in the small houses. How they enjoyed using the jargon of these women! But it surprised him that a student did tour the neighborhood in earnest as a mimic.

"Who are your favorite actors, Otama-san?" Suezo said, turning to her suddenly.

"I don't have any favorites," she said. She had been quietly listening to the conversation.

"Oh!" interrupted her father, "she's never been inside a theatre!" And he added: "We live right next to one, and all the girls on our block go to see the plays. But not my Otama. Never. I hear the other girls rush out of their houses the minute they catch the first note!"

The old man, in spite of his intentions, was apt to revert to the praise of his daughter.

CHAPTER EIGHT

THEY REACHED an agreement. Otama would live in the house Suezo had bought on Muenzaka.

But the transfer, which Suezo had thought a simple matter, raised some difficulties.

"I want my father as close as possible," Otama had said. "I want to visit him often. I must look after him."

Her original intention had been to send her father, already over sixty, the greater part of her allowance and to provide him with a young maid who would make him comfortable. If her plan worked, he would no longer have to remain in their dismal home, its wall shared with that of a rickshaw garage. "Why can't you put my father in a house near my own?" she had asked.

So it turned out that Suezo, who had thought that all he need do was to receive his mistress in the house he had purchased for her, now had, in addition, just as he had been forced to invite the father with the daughter at their first interview, to undertake the problem of the old man's living quarters.

She had told Suezo: "It's my own concern. I don't want to trouble you."

But since she had mentioned the problem, he could not avoid it. He wanted to show her how generous he was.

Finally Suezo had said: "Look. When you come to live at Muenzaka, I'll rent a house for your father at Ike-no-hata."

It had been forced on him. When Suezo saw how Otama would have to save and pinch on her allowance after she had said that she would manage the arrangement herself, he couldn't allow her to do so.

Thus Suezo had to pay more than he had calculated. But he paid without bitterness, much to the bewilderment of the old go-between.

By the middle of July, Otama and her father had settled in their new homes. Suezo was so bewitched by the modesty of the girl's manner and her maidenly way of speaking that he visited her almost every night. He had been capable of complete ruthlessness in his dealings, and still was, but now he tried every trick of tenderness to gain Otama's affection. This, I believe, is what historians have often called the touch of weakness in a man of iron will.

On these visits Suezo made it a point to appear almost every evening, though he never stayed the entire night. With the help of the go-between, Otama had hired a maid. Ume was only thirteen, and she did the kitchen work, which, Otama could not help feeling, was little more than having a child play a pleasant game. The result was that Otama did not have enough to do during the day and was left without anyone to talk to.

She would find herself wishing for her master to come earlier in the evening and would smile at the change taking place in herself. Before, the situation had been different. She had also been alone while her father was out selling his candies, but during his absence she had taken in piece-work. She had not even had the friendship of the girls in the neighborhood, yet she had never regretted the loss, had never even been bored. She would think only of the sum she would receive upon completing the task. There would be her father's surprise, his smile of pleasure because of her diligence. Yes, she had worked hard in those days. But now it was different, and she was beginning to feel the pains of ennui.

Yet her weariness was not unbearable, relieved as it was by Suezo's evening calls. Her father's position in the new house was a more difficult one than her own. Overnight he had been given luxuries he had never had before. At odd times during the day he would say to himself: "Am I bewitched? Yes! Bewitched by a fox!"

But the change was not enough to satisfy him, and he began to miss those earlier days when he and Otama would spend their evenings together, the oil lamp lit, their small talk about the ways of the world begun, the silence without disturbance from others infiltrating their room.

"A pretty dream that was," said the old man to himself. "It'll never come back."

At other times he said to himself: "When will she come? I expect her. But when?"

A number of days had passed since their separation, and he had not received even a short visit from her.

For the first few days the old man was delighted with the house, the maid from the country, the conveniences. The girl cooked his meals and did the heavy task of carrying in the water from the well. He tried to keep busy too and helped the girl put the rooms in order. Sometimes he swept. Occasionally he sent her out to shop for him. And in the evening when he heard her working in the kitchen, he sprinkled the ground around the parasol pine. Later, his figure framed in the low window, his arms on the sill, a pipe in his mouth, he watched the movements of the noisy crows over Ueno Hill and looked at the shrine on the wooded island in the pond, the lotus flowers in the water blurred by degrees in the thickening haze of evening.

He said to himself that he was grateful for his good fortune, that he was satisfied with his circumstances, yet at the same time he could not help thinking: "I raised her without anyone's help. I kept her from the moment she was born. We didn't even need words. We could understand each other without talk. A daughter who was always kind, always waiting for me when I came home."

He would sit at the window for hours, his eyes on the pond or the people walking along the street.

At times he wanted to shout: "Otama! Look at that! Did you see that carp jump?"

When a stranger was passing, he wanted to call his daughter to the window, wanted to tell her: "A foreigner! What a hat she's got on! A whole bird on top of it!"

How he wished he could say that to Otama, to cry: "Did you ever see such a sight?"

And it pained him that he could not. *loss of innocence, a child leaves,*

With each passing day he became increasingly irritable. He began to find fault with the maid when she brought him his meals. He had not had a servant for many years, and since he was a tender-hearted man, he refrained from scolding her. But he was uneasy in her presence, for no matter what she did, it went against him. To do justice to the girl—just up to Tokyo from the country—it was unfortunate for her to be compared with Otama, who bore herself so well and did everything gently and quietly.

Finally, on the fourth day after moving to his new house, he was shocked to find that the maid had her thumb in his soup as she brought it to him at breakfast.

"No more serving me! Go away!" He found the courage to say that much.

After the meal he took his usual position at the window. He didn't think it would rain, and with the weather so cool, he thought he would go out for a walk. As he went around the pond he kept speculating: "She may come while I'm out."

And he turned several times to look at his house.

Eventually he came to a small bridge leading towards Muenzaka. Should he go to his daughter's house? But he couldn't bring himself to take that direction. It seemed as though he felt hindered by a barrier suddenly rising between him and his daughter, an awareness of their altered positions, something. A mother might never have such a feeling towards an only child. Wondering why a father should, he continued around the pond instead of crossing the bridge. Suddenly he discovered he was standing in front of Suezo's place. The go-between had previously pointed to it from his own house. From close up, it seemed better looking, surrounded by its high mud wall with bamboo strips nailed diagonally at the top of the barrier. The neighboring house, which he had been told belonged to the scholar Fukuchi, had more extensive grounds, but the residence itself was old-fashioned and not as gaudy and pretentious as Suezo's.

For a while the old man stood in front of Suezo's house, his eyes on the service gate of white woodwork, yet his mind definite that he did not want to enter it.

The old man was not thinking of anything in particular, but for some time he seemed dazed, attacked by a rush of feeling, a kind of loneliness coming over him and mixed with the sudden awareness of life's brevity, its change. If you force me to define these emotions more specifically, they were those of a parent who has debased himself by selling his daughter as a mistress.

A week passed, and still Otama had not come. He was annoyed at himself for wanting to see her so badly, and he wondered: "Has she forgotten me? She's comfortable now. Why not?"

These suspicions were so faint that he alone could have brought them about and played with them in his own mind. Suspicions they were, and yet not such as to make him hate her. But superficially at least, with the irony that one often uses in conversation, he murmured: "I'd be happier if I could."

Then his reasoning took another direction: "I leave the house so that I don't have to think too much. Let her come when I'm not there! She'll be sorry she missed me. But what if she doesn't care if I'm out? Well, at least her visit was a waste of time. That should annoy her. It would

42

serve her right too!" And on his walks he repeated these conclusions a number of times.

He would go to the park, rest on a bench in the shade, and then get up and walk again. If he happened to see a covered rickshaw, he would say to himself: "Ah! she's visited me! Oh, she'll be upset all right not to find me in. That'll teach her!" And if, as he half wished, it did punish her, he knew that he was also putting himself to a test.

In the evening he began to go to the theatre to listen to the storyteller and the recitations of dramatic ballads. Inside, he imagined his daughter on one of her futile visits to his house, but the thought would suddenly occur to him that she was also in the hall, and he would look around at the young women with the same hair style as Otama's. Once he was certain he had seen her. The woman had entered during the intermission, her companion in *yukata* and with a panama hat, quite a new fashion in those days. The old man watched her take a seat in the gallery, put her hands on the railing, and look down into the pit below. But as he looked more closely, he said to himself: "No, her face is too round. Besides, she's smaller than Otama." In addition, her escort was accompanied not only by that woman but by others who sat behind him.

They were all geisha girls and apprentices.

And he heard a student near him whisper: "That's Fukuchi!"

As Otama's father left the hall after the performance, he saw the man followed by his troop of geishas and novices and led by a woman holding a long-handled lantern with the name of the theatre written in red characters.

He walked on in the same direction as this party, sometimes going ahead, sometimes falling behind.

At last he reached his own house and went in.

CHAPTER NINE

OTAMA, who had never been away from her father, was eager to know how he was. Yet, in spite of this desire, several days had passed without her being able to visit him. She was afraid that Suezo might come when she was out, and she feared that he would be annoyed if he did not find her. Usually he came at night and stayed until eleven, but he began to appear briefly at odd hours.

The first time he came during the day he said, sitting down opposite her in front of the charcoal brazier: "I've dropped in on my way to an appointment. I'll just smoke a cigarette and go."

As a matter of fact, Otama seldom knew when he would come, so she didn't have the courage to leave. She might have slipped out in the morning, but she considered Ume an unreliable child. Moreover, Otama didn't want to be seen then or in the afternoon, for she didn't like the thought of the neighbors staring at her. She was so shy that at first she went to the bathhouse below the slope only after she had sent Ume out to see that it was not crowded.

To make matters worse, on the third day after she had moved in, she had been frightened. She was already timid enough to give the situation more attention than it deserved. On first moving into Muenzaka, she had been called on by the vegetable dealer and the fishmonger. When she agreed to be their customer, they gave her an account book. On the day in question, when the fish had not been delivered, she sent Ume down the slope to get a few slices for lunch. Otama was not used to eating fish every day, having taken her meals without such delicacies. Nor had her father been particular about food as long as she had prepared it well and it was healthy for him. But once she had heard one of her neighbors at their old house saying that she and her father had bought no fish for several days. Remembering how embarrassed she had been then, Otama decided to send the girl for some. "If Ume thinks I'm trying to save money," she reasoned, "then I'm being unfair to Suezo. He's not like that."

But a short while later the maid returned crying.

"What is it? Tell me," Otama said a number of times before the girl would speak.

"I went into a fish market, but not the one we buy from. I looked around but couldn't see the dealer. And I thought: 'Why, he's probably calling on customers after buying fresh fish at the waterfront.' And then I saw some mackerel looking like they'd just been pulled out of the water. 'How much?' I ask the wife. 'I've never seen you around here,' she says to me, not even telling me how much. 'Whose house you from?' she asks. And when I told her, she began to make a face like she was angry. 'Why!' she says. 'Then I'm sorry for you. Go on back where you're from and tell your mistress we don't sell fish to the—whore of a usurer!' And then she turned her back on me, smoking her pipe, pretending I wasn't even there!"

Ume had been too shocked and hurt to go to another shop and had run all the way back. And the simple girl, all the while making sympathetic gestures, told her mistress the entire story line by line.

As Ume spoke, Otama's face turned pale, and for a while she could not answer. A mixture of feelings tumbled inside the inexperienced girl. It was impossible for her to disentangle her confused thoughts, but the total confusion put so heavy a strain upon the heart of a pure girl sold that all her blood seemed to be drawn into it, draining the color from her face and leaving her back chilled with cold perspiration.

On these occasions an insignificant thought seems to take hold of us. Would Ume continue to serve her after this disgrace?

the woman symbolizes social acceptance she sells food - social vitality

loss of innocence

45

As the girl watched Otama, she could see that her words had upset her mistress. But she could not guess what had caused Otama such dismay. The girl had returned to the house in a fit, but now it seemed that the food for lunch was indispensable, and she still carried the coins in the folds of her sash.

"I never met such a nasty person!" Ume said, a look of compassion on her face. "Why! who'd shop at such a place? Not me. There's another shop up ahead of that one. Near a fox-shrine. That's where I'll go. And right away too." And she got up from the mats to run out.

Otama gave her an automatic smile and a nod, moved at finding a friend in Ume, who hurried out of the room.

Otama remained seated. As the strain became less intense, she began to cry quietly and reached into her kimono sleeve for a handkerchief. She heard a voice cry out: "It's not fair! How cruel!" It was her own confusion. By these words she did not mean that she hated the woman who refused to sell her the fish, nor did she feel sad or mortified in recognizing that her status had barred her from a simple fish market. She did not even feel resentment toward Suezo, who had purchased her and who had now turned out to be a usurer. It was humiliating to belong to such a man, but she did not even feel that. She had heard that usurers were disgusting persons, looked down on, feared, detested. But her father's only experience in that direction had been with pawnbrokers. And when their clerks had not been kind enough to give him the sum he needed, he had never complained in spite of the inconvenience. So, even though she had been told that such men existed, her fear was similar to that of a child toward an ogre or a policeman—not a particularly keen one. What then was this despair she suddenly felt?

In her feeling, the sense of injustice done by the world in general and men in particular was almost absent. If she had such a sense, it was that of the unfairness of her

46

own destiny. She had done nothing wrong, yet she was to be persecuted by the world. This pained her. This was her despair. When she had learned that the policeman had deceived her and deserted her, she had used the same words for the first time in her life: "It's not fair! How cruel!" And she had used them again when she had been forced into becoming a mistress. And now that she realized she was not only a "whore" but one kept by a usurer whom the world detested, the feeling of humiliation that time and resignation had softened and toned down emerged once more with its sharp outline and strong colors. This was the substance of Otama's emotion, if you force me to describe it in any reasonable way.

Eventually she stood up, opened a closet, and from a bag of imitation leather took out a calico apron which she had made. Tying the apron around her waist, she entered the kitchen with a sigh. Her silk apron was more like a dress, and she never used it while working there. She was so fond of personal cleanliness that even when she wore an easy-to-wash summer kimono she would tie a towel around her hair in order to keep the neckband from getting soiled.

Gradually her thoughts settled. Resignation was the mental attitude she had most experienced. And in this direction her mind adjusted itself like a well-oiled machine.

CHAPTER TEN

ONE EVENING when Suezo came, he took his usual seat opposite Otama. From their first meeting in her new home she had put a cushion beside the charcoal brazier as soon as she knew he was there. He would go to it and sit down, and relaxing with his pipe, engage in small talk. From her own position on the mats she would answer him in monosyllables. She would say a few words, pass her hands along the frame of the brazier, toy with the charcoal tongs, do anything to keep herself busy. If she hadn't had a definite place before the brazier, she wouldn't have known what to do. It may be said that she was facing a formidable enemy with only the battlement of the brazier to protect her.

During their talks Suezo would get her to speak for a time, usually on trivial and sentimental matters about the years she had lived alone with her father. In spite of himself, Suezo would listen with a smile, not so much to what she was saying but rather to the pleasant melody of her voice. It was as though he were hearing the pure tones of a bell-insect. Then Otama would suddenly become self-conscious, blush at having run on about herself, and dash off the rest of her sentence before lapsing into her usual silence. With his penetration Suezo could see that her speech and behavior were so totally innocent that she seemed as transparent as fresh water in the bottom of a flat vase. His delight in their conversation was equal to his own joy in soaking his limbs in an agreeably warm bath after an exhausting day at work. The experience of this delight, quite a new one for him, had been giving him unconsciously a sort of "culture" since the start of his visits to her. After all, a primitive beast can be subdued by sensitive hands.

But a number of days after she had moved in, he became aware of her increasing restlessness. When he took his place before the brazier, she would get up, find some unnecessary task to do, occupy her hands. From the beginning of their relationship, she had avoided his glance and had hesitated in answering his questions. On this occasion her conduct was so strange that there had to be some explanation for it.

"Come now," he said, filling his pipe, "something's bothering you. What is it?"

"No," said Otama, her eyes widening, "there's nothing wrong."

She had pulled out one of the drawers from the frame of the brazier as if to arrange it, but she had already put it in order. She began to search for an item when obviously she had nothing to look for. Suezo could tell that her eyes could not keep very great secrets.

In spite of frowning unconsciously, he brightened instantly. "Come, Otama, you know you're worried. It's written all over your face. I can just make out the words. Let me see," he said, looking at her sharply. "Oh yes! 'I'm all confused. What'll I do? What'll I do?'"

Otama was embarrassed, and for a while she sat in silence as though she did not know how to begin. Suezo could clearly perceive the motion of this delicate instrument.

"I—well—it's my father. I've been thinking about visiting him—one of these days. . . . And it's been long since. . . ."

Though a man may see the particular movement of a highly intricate machine, he may not necessarily understand its total operation. An insect that must always ward off persecution from the bigger and stronger of the species is given the gift of mimicry. A woman tells lies.

"What!" said Suezo, smiling in spite of his scolding tone. "You haven't visited him yet? His house right at Ike-no-hata? In front of your nose? Why, just think of Iwasaki's estate on the other side. It's almost as if the two of you were living in the same house. If you wish, we'll go now, though tomorrow would be better."

"But—I've so many things to think of—to consider," she said, poking the ashes with the charcoal tongs and stealing a glance at him.

"Nonsense!" he interrupted. "Such a simple thing doesn't require a reason! What an infant you are!" he said, his voice nevertheless tender.

49

The matter ended there. Later, he even said with humorous gallantry: "If it's so much trouble, I'll come around in the morning and take you. After all, it *is* several hundred yards!"

Lately Otama had tried to think of him in several ways. When she saw him in front of her with his reliable and considerate manner, even tenderness, she wondered why he had chosen a base profession. And she said to herself: "I may change him, make him find something else to do." But she knew this was more than she could do. And yet she confessed to herself: "He's not detestable! Usurer or not, he's not detestable!"

As for Suezo, he had caught an image at the bottom of Otama's mind, had sounded her out regarding it, and had found it a childish trifle. But as he walked down Muenzaka after eleven that night, it seemed as though something were behind what he had already discovered. He was shrewd enough to locate part of the trouble. "Something," he conjectured, "someone's told her something. Something about me. And she's holding it against me."

But he did not know who had told what.

CHAPTER ELEVEN

WHEN OTAMA reached her father's house the next morning, he had just finished breakfast. She had never spent a great deal of time getting ready to go out, and she hurried along thinking that perhaps she had come too early, but the old man, not a late sleeper, had already swept the entrance to his house and had sprinkled water over the grounds. And after washing his hands and feet, he was just taking his lonely meal on the new mats.

A few doors from her father's house, some places where

50

geishas entertained had recently been constructed, and on certain evenings the neighborhood was noisy. But the houses to the right and left of the old man's, like his own, kept their doors closed and were quiet, especially in the morning.

As the old man looked out of his low window, he could see through the branches of the parasol pine in his front garden the string-like willow trees faintly moving in the fresh breeze. Beyond them the lotus leaves covered the pond, their green color spotted here and there with light pink flowers blooming at that early hour. In the winter the old man's house would be cold since it faced north, but in the summer it was as good as any one could wish to find.

Ever since Otama had been old enough to think for herself, she had hoped that if the opportunity arose she would do one thing or another for her father. And when she saw the house he was living in, she couldn't restrain her joy, couldn't help feeling her prayers realized. But even the happiness she felt had its bitter ingredient, an awareness of her altered position. "If I could see my father without that," she said to herself, "how happy I could be!"

She felt the frustration expressed in the proverb: "An unfulfilled wish is the world's way."

The old man had put down his chopsticks and was taking his tea when he heard a noise at the front door. Since it had never been opened by a visitor, he was surprised. And setting aside his teacup, he kept his eyes in that direction. He could not see anyone behind the folding screen of rush stalks, but when he heard his daughter call: "Otossan," he had a difficult time remaining seated instead of jumping up and rushing over to meet her. Yet he sat where he was, his mind busily trying to find the words to use and thinking he would begin with "It's a wonder you still remember your father!" But when he saw Otama hurry toward him, her face radiant as though experiencing a relief from pain after the interval of their separation, he couldn't have said those words. Yet he was dissatisfied with his weakness in not being able to say even that much, and he stared at her face in silence.

Yes, he thought, she was beautiful. Even when he had been poor, he had insisted that this only source of pride should always look her best, and he had even refused to let her do heavy tasks. But now that he was seeing her for the first time after an absence of ten days, she seemed reborn. Compared to the present Otama, who was consciously grooming and polishing herself, the daughter he remembered was a precious stone in the rough. A parent who sees his own daughter or an old man who sees a young girl cannot deny the beauty of a beautiful object. And such men cannot be exempt from feeling the power that beauty has in easing the heart.

The old man had consciously remained silent, had intended to make her see that he was sullen, but he couldn't help himself and softened against his will. Even Otama, who had never known a day of separation from her father before this new arrangement and who had not seen him for ten days, was speechless for a moment. She had much to tell him, but all she could do was look at his face with pleasure.

"Are you finished?" asked the maid, her tone quick and her voice rising as she appeared suddenly at the entrance to the kitchen.

Otama couldn't catch the girl's words. And when the maid, her hair rolled up around a comb so that it was out of proportion to her fat face, saw Otama, she stared at the visitor rudely.

"Take it away! And bring in fresh tea! Use the green on the shelf," the old man said, pushing the tray forward for her to take it into the kitchen.

"Oh, you don't have to trouble her to make special tea for me."

"What kind of nonsense is that! I've got some cake too." He went over to the closet and, taking out a tin of egg-crackers, put some into a cake dish.

"There's a baker not too far from here who makes these. And guess what? You can buy Joen's cooked fish in soy sauce in an alley right next to it!"

"Ah, Joen! Do you remember, Otossan, when you took me to the music hall? And Joen was there? Talking about a feast he went to, saying the fish was as good as his own. And how we laughed! What a pleasingly plump man he was! Coming on stage and flinging up his kimono before sitting down. I could hardly keep myself from laughing out loud. I wish you'd get that fat!"

"What? Be as fat as him? Not me!" he said, putting the dish before her. Soon the maid brought the tea, and the father and daughter were talking as easily as if they had done the same thing yesterday and the day before.

"How are you getting along?" he asked suddenly, feeling the awkwardness of the question. "Does Suezo come dropping in every so often?"

"Yes—" she said, hesitating, not knowing what to reply. Suezo came not merely "often" but every night. If she had been Suezo's wife and someone had asked her how she was getting on with her husband, she would have said happily: "Wonderfully! Please don't worry about us." But since she was his mistress, her conscience prevented her from revealing Suezo's nightly appearance.

"We're managing," she said after a pause. "You shouldn't worry about me. Please don't."

"Everything's all right then—" His daughter's reply had not quite satisfied him, and the two of them unconsciously began speaking as though their mouths were full of paste. They had never kept anything from each other, but now they were speaking with formality, like unrelated

53

persons having secrets to conceal from each other. When the policeman had duped them and they had felt embarrassed in the presence of their neighbors, they still had the greatest confidence in one another, convinced as they were that what had happened was not their fault. Yet this situation was different, for after the desperate decision that had put them in comfortable positions, they became painfully aware of a barrier thrown across their former intimacy.

A few moments of silence followed. The old man wanted a more definite answer and approached the question in a new way. "What sort of man is he?"

"Let me see," said Otama, inclining her head to the side almost as though she were speaking to herself. "I guess that after everything's said, he's not a bad man. He hasn't said anything cruel—though it's only been a few days."

The old man looked puzzled. "Hum—why should he be a *bad* man?"

She looked at her father, her heartbeat increasing. She realized that she now had her chance to tell him what she had learned, yet it pained her to bring him any new problems. She had put him at ease now. He was comfortable. And she suddenly decided: "I won't tell him!" She would keep the matter to herself, an unopened secret behind the one they shared of her serving as a mistress, even though in doing this she was aware that the gap between them was widening.

She diverged from the point, saying: "It's just that I heard he made his money in a clever way by doing various things. And that made me anxious about the kind of man he was. Well, what should I say about him? Oh . . . he looks like a gentleman. I don't know whether he's really one or not. Still it seems to me that he tries to say and do things so that other people will think he is.

54

And, Otossan, isn't it better to try to be that kind of man even if it's only a matter of trying?"

After this speech she looked up at her father. However honest a woman may be, she feels less hesitation than a man in keeping back what is really on her mind at the moment and speaking about other things. And it may be said that those women who speak the most at such times are the more honest of their sex.

"Well, you may be right. But you talk as though you don't trust him."

"Ah, I'm getting smarter," she said with a smile, "bit by bit. From now on I'm not going to be made a fool of. Don't you think I'm a brave woman?"

These pointed remarks of opposition directed at him from the daughter he thought invariably meek surprised the old man, and he gazed at her with misgivings.

"Well, Otama," he said, "I've lived and been made a fool of all my life. But you know, you're better off being cheated than cheating. I don't care what situation a person's in, he has to pay back what he owes someone else. You've got to be faithful to your obligations."

"You never have to worry about that, Otossan. How often you used to say: 'Ta-bo's honest.' I know I am. But lately I've made up my mind, and I won't let myself be tricked again. I won't lie to anyone. I won't deceive anyone. But at the same time no one's going to deceive me either. I'll see to it that they don't."

"All of this, I suppose, means that you don't trust Suezo?"

"Just that. He treats me as though I were an infant. I'm not surprised that his type takes that approach with me. He thinks he can go through somebody's eye and nose without being seen. But I'm not as much of a child as that."

"You don't mean that he's lied to you?"

behavior is predicated on social acceptability

"Yes, he has. You remember, the go-between said he was a widower left with some children and that the woman he took under his care would be just like his wife though not in name. She said that it was only because of what the neighbors would say about our living in a poor district that he couldn't marry me. Well, he has a wife. He told me so himself. He didn't even hesitate. He didn't even feel ashamed. I was shocked."

The old man was shocked too. "Is it true? Then—then what she said was only a matchmaker's trick?"

"So I must be kept strictly secret from his wife. Since he's lying to her, how can I trust him completely?"

Otama seemed to have risen in the old man's estimation, and he looked at her so absent-mindedly that he forgot to knock out the ashes in his pipe.

"I've got to go back now," Otama said, as though she had suddenly remembered something. "Since I've found my way here once, it'll be easy to come again. From now on I'll visit almost every day. The reason I haven't been here sooner was that I didn't think it right to come until Suezo made the suggestion. But last night I finally told him that I wanted to visit you and got his consent. And so here I am today! My maid's really a child. She can't even prepare lunch without my help."

"Well, if you got his permission, eat here."

"No, I don't feel safe about my house. I'll come again —very soon. Goodbye, Otossan."

When she stood up to leave, the maid rushed to the entrance to put her wooden clogs in the right direction. Even an ignorant woman has to make observations on any woman she comes across. A certain philosopher once said that one of that sex regards another she meets, if only on the street and for the first time, as a rival. And this country wench, who constantly put her thumb into a bowl of soup, seemed to have been eavesdropping on Otama, who was too beautiful to ignore.

"All right then," said Otama's father, remaining seated on his cushion. "Come soon. And give my regards to Suezo."

Otama took a small wallet from the layers of her black sash and gave the maid some money wrapped in paper, put on her low clogs, and left the house.

She had entered the gate with the intention of revealing her troubles to her father and gaining a partner in her misery, but she came out in high spirits that seemed strange even to herself. While she had talked to him, she was conscious of trying to appear strong and firm instead of adding any anxieties to the freedom he had found, and she sensed the release of some hidden quality in her. Previously she had depended on others, but now she knew the power of an unexpected self-reliance. And as she walked around the pond, she felt cheered.

Already high above Ueno Hill, the sun blazed with its heat and dyed the Benten Shrine on the pond's inner island a deeper red. In spite of the hot glare Otama walked on without opening the small parasol that she carried.

CHAPTER TWELVE

ONE NIGHT after his return from Muenzaka, Suezo found his wife, Otsune, sitting up alone after the children at her side had fallen asleep. Her usual practice was to doze off with them. On this occasion she knew her husband had come in under the mosquito net. She didn't turn her head toward him but kept it bent down.

His bed was laid out farther back near the wall and away from the other members of the family. A cushion, smoking set, and tea things had been arranged beside his pillow. He sat down, lit a cigarette over the charcoal fire in the smoking set, and said tenderly: "What's wrong? You're still awake?"

His wife said nothing.

Since she refused to accept this proposal of peace from him, he wouldn't make any further concessions. And deliberately ignoring her, he leaned back smoking.

"Where you been till now?" she asked, suddenly lifting her head and looking at him. Since they had hired a maid, her speech had gradually improved, but when alone with her husband, she lapsed into former vulgarities.

Suezo looked at her sharply, but remained silent. He realized that she had learned something, but since he couldn't measure its range, he could say nothing yet. He wasn't the kind of man who gives bait for the opposition's advantage.

"Now I know everything!" she cried, her voice shrill and trembling at the end of her words to the point of tears.

"You sound so mysterious. What do you know?" he said, like a man who is surprised by the unexpected but who still retains a gentle tone.

"You ask too much of a person! How can you pretend like that? Even without any shame!" Her husband's calm so excited her that her voice broke, and she was forced to wipe her eyes on the sleeve of her underwear.

"I still don't understand what you're talking about. Tell me what's on your mind. I can't even guess."

"Ah! Is that all you can say when I'm asking you where you been tonight? How could you do such a thing? Keeping a whore, telling me you got work to do!" Her red, flat-nosed face looked as if it had been boiled in tears, and a lock of hair was stuck to her cheek. Her wet, narrow eyes opened as wide as possible, and she looked directly into his face. Suddenly she crawled over and grabbed the hand holding his cigarette.

"Stop it!" he said, shaking her off. He put out the ashes that were scattered over the mats. But she grabbed

58

his arm again and cried: "Is there another person like you in the whole world? You've made a lot of money, but is there anyone else who dresses up like a gentleman and leaves his wife with nothing? Without even a kimono? Letting her take care of the children! Yet—yet so conceited that he takes up with a whore!" *expectation, result*

"Quit that crying! Do you hear?" Once more he brushed her hand away. "You'll wake the children. And your voice is carrying to the maid's room!" His wife could feel the force behind these whispered words.

Suddenly the younger child turned and spoke in his sleep, and Suezo's wife was forced to lower her voice. "After all," she said, pressing her face against her husband's chest and weeping silently, "what can I do?"

"You don't have to do a thing. Someone's got you all excited. Who told you I had a mistress or some secret woman or such nonsense?" As he spoke, he noticed her tangled hair against his body, and he speculated on a question one usually considers at a more leisurely moment: Why does an ugly woman insist on arranging her hair in a way that fits only a beautiful one? As the movement of her hair against him became less, he could at the same time feel the pressure from her heavy breasts, which had supplied ample nourishment for each of their children. "Who told you?" he asked again.

"Forget about that so long as it's true." The pressure of her breasts increased.

"But it's not true, so I do mind who's misinformed you. Tell me."

"All right. The wife of the fish dealer—Uwokin."

"What? What? I can't understand you chattering away like a monkey! Who's that? Who?"

Otsune pulled herself away from him and smiled in spite of herself.

"Uwokin's wife."

"That woman! Just as I thought." He took another

59

cigarette and gazed tenderly at his wife's frantic face. "A newspaper is said to form the public's opinion against a particular person, but I've never seen it done. Maybe that gossip has done just that. She meddles with everything in the neighborhood. Who'd believe her words? Listen to me. I'll tell you the truth."

His wife felt as though she were stumbling in a fog, yet she wondered if she weren't being duped by his words, and she remained alert. Watching him closely, she tried to follow him carefully. But when her husband used the difficult words of a newspaper as he had done in speaking about public opinion, she was overwhelmed and submitted without comprehension.

He fixed his sympathetic face close to his wife's and, occasionally drawing on his cigarette, went on: "Well, do you remember that student Yoshida who used to visit us so often? Wears glasses with gold rims and silk clothes? He's working at Chiba now—in a hospital. But he still owes me more than he can pay in two or three years. He's become intimate with a woman he met while he was still a student at the dormitory. Up to a short while ago he kept her in a rented house in Nanamagari. Well, at the beginning he sent her a monthly allowance. But since the first of the year, she hasn't received even a note. So she came to me and asked me to get in touch with him for her. You might well wonder I know her! Yoshida told me to come over to Nanamagari to renew our agreement. He's afraid that if he comes here too often some of his friends will recognize him. And that's how she got to know me. I was embarrassed enough by what she asked me to do, but I took the trouble to look into this along with my own business. And it's still not settled. And the woman keeps begging me for things. Now I'm sorry to have gotten into this mess. It's getting to be more than I can handle. There was the question of money, and besides that, she asked me to find her a comfortable house—

not too much rent—so I took the time to move her to a house that used to belong to the parents of a pawnbroker at Kiridoshi. What with this and that, I've stopped in at her new place several times for a smoke or two. And I guess that gave the neighbors something to talk about. A sewing teacher lives next door, and several young girls meet there. Naturally they like to gossip. Who'd be fool enough to hide a mistress in such a place?" He laughed contemptuously.

Suezo's wife had listened carefully, and a glow came into her small eyes. "Well," she said coquettishly, "maybe what you say's true, but you can't tell about visiting that kind of woman so often. I'm sure she'll give herself to any man for money."

"Don't talk as though you were stupid! Am I the kind of man who would make love to another woman when I have *you* for my wife? Can you point to a single time when I had anything to do with anyone else? We're too old to be jealous of each other. Isn't that so? Listen here! You'd better not go too far with this!"

Suezo sang a song of triumph in his heart, for his explanation had been more effective than he had hoped.

"But I can't help worrying. Women like your type."

"Nonsense! That's what people call adoring one's own idol."

"What?"

"I mean—you're the only one who likes me. Why! It's already past one. Come on, let's go to bed."

CHAPTER THIRTEEN

Suezo's explanation, a mixture of truth and fiction, reduced his wife's jealousy temporarily, but since its effect was naturally only palliative, the gossip and grumbling never stopped as long as the woman lived at Muenzaka. Even the maid told Suezo's wife about the scandal, saying among other things at different times: "Today, so-and-so saw our master go there." But Suezo was never at a loss for an excuse.

"Do you have to work at night?" his wife often asked him doubtfully.

"Who'd want to talk about loans in the early hours of the morning?" he retorted.

"But why," she continued, "didn't that kind of thing go on at night before this?"

"Because now my business is bigger."

Formerly Suezo had managed all the transactions by himself. Now, however, in addition to an office near his home, he had set up a kind of branch office at Ryusenji-machi in order to save the students time by letting them borrow money there instead of taking the long walk to his home. If a student wanted some money for a licensed prostitute at Nezu, he ran to Suezo's main office, but if he desired a Yoshiwara woman, he went to the branch office. And later on, by contacting this office, a student who wished to spend a night of rioting at the Nishinomiya, a restaurant in the Yoshiwara, could do so without paying if he had Suezo's permission. It was, so to speak, a commissariat organized at the frontier of debauchery.

About a month had passed without Suezo and his wife colliding into any battles. Until then his sophistry had been effective, but it was broken through from an unexpected quarter.

One cool morning when Suezo remained at home, Otsune and her maid went shopping. But as they were returning, the maid, who had been following her mistress, suddenly pulled at Otsune's sleeve.

"What are you up to?" Otsune demanded, her tone sharp and her eyes turning on the maid. But the servant stood silently and pointed to a young woman loitering in front of a shop on the left side of the street. Annoyed, Otsune looked in the direction indicated, but unconsciously she stopped short. At the same time the other woman turned around. She and Otsune stared at each other.

At first Otsune thought she was a geisha. "If she is," she said to herself as a first impression, "then no single geisha in Sukiya-machi can match her in beauty!" But a moment later Otsune noticed that this woman lacked something that every geisha has—something that she was unable to define herself. If it could be described, I might explain it as exaggerated behavior. A geisha may dress herself in excellent taste, but it is more or less excessive. And this added quality deprives her of a certain degree of moderation, of gentility. Otsune felt that the other woman lacked this element of exaggerated behavior.

The woman in front of the shop, faintly conscious of some passerby stopping, had looked around. But not noticing anything special about the stranger, she had once more turned, and with her parasol propped between her knees, which were pulled inward, she looked for some small silver coins in the purse she had withdrawn from her sash.

The shop, on the southern side of Naka-cho, was called Tashigaraya, an unusual name that was parodied in an anonymous and satiric poem, for when it was read backwards it referred to an indecent act. Among the shop's goods was a kind of toothpowder packaged in a red paper bag with characters printed in gold. At that time toothpaste had not yet been imported, and this product was known for its smooth quality. After her early morning visit to her father, Otama had stopped to purchase some of it on the way home.

When Otsune had passed Otama by some several steps, her maid whispered: "Okusan! that's the woman of Mu-enzaka!" Otsune nodded silently, but the maid seemed disappointed, as though her words had no effect.

When Otsune had concluded that the woman was not a geisha, she had instinctively said: "Ah, the Muenzaka woman!" This intuition was aided by her recognition that the maid would not have tugged at her sleeve merely for the sake of calling her attention to a beautiful woman, but another unexpected item had influenced her: the parasol between Otama's knees.

A little more than a month ago, Otsune's husband had brought her a parasol as a gift on his return from Yokohama, one with a long handle out of proportion to the spread of the cloth. It would have been all right for a tall foreigner to toy with, but when the squat Otsune carried it, it resembled, to make an extreme comparison, a swaddling cloth attached to the top of a clothesrod. So Otsune had never used it. Its cloth was of white ground with a fine checkered pattern dyed in indigo. And Otsune had immediately recognized that the woman standing in front of the Tashigaraya owned the same kind of parasol.

Otsune and her maid turned toward the pond at the corner of a saké dealer's shop, and the maid said propitiatingly: "You see, Okusan, she's not a very pretty woman. Her face is flat and she's too tall!"

"You shouldn't speak ill of a person." This, said in a reprimanding tone, was the sole answer the maid got from her mistress, who walked on quickly. The maid followed with an injured expression on her face.

Otsune was inwardly raging. She was unable to think clearly. As she walked toward her house, she didn't know how to approach her husband or what to say to him, yet she felt compelled to attack him somehow, to speak, to say something. How delighted she had been when he had brought her that parasol, when he had actually given it to her! "I always had to ask for something from him," she thought. And when he had said: "For you. Take it," she couldn't help asking herself: "What's this for? Why's he turned kind so suddenly?" Now she knew that he had given it to her as an afterthought. That woman had asked him for one—she was certain of that now. And knowing nothing, she had thanked him, thanked him for a parasol she couldn't even use! "And not only that," she said to herself, "but he gave her that kimono and those ornaments in her hair. He gave them to her!"

Otsune glanced at her own sateen parasol. How different it was from that other one of foreign make! "Everything I'm wearing is different from hers!"

Nor did Otsune merely worry about herself. "A tight-sleeved kimono will do for the boy," Suezo had said. "As for the girl, don't waste money by dressing her up now. She's too young."

Were ever the wife and children of a man worth thousands and thousands of yen so poorly dressed as she and her children? And she thought that if Suezo had neglected them, that woman was to blame. Of course everything he had told her about Yoshida was a lie. And when Suezo had said: "She used to live at Nanamagari," he had been keeping her even then. Yes, that was the truth. He had made excuses for his own clothing and personal items, saying: "I have my position to think of," and Otsune thought how she might have said: "Yes, you have your woman to think of!"

He had taken that woman all over, but he had taken his own wife nowhere. "How unfair! And cruel!" she whispered.

Otsune was lost in these thoughts when she suddenly heard her maid cry out: "Why! where are you going, Okusan?"

Otsune stopped, startled. She had been walking with her head down and was about to pass her own house.

The maid laughed rudely.

CHAPTER FOURTEEN

Suezo had been at home reading his newspaper and smoking when Otsune went out shopping after clearing away the breakfast things, but when she returned, he was no longer there. This disappointed her, for on entering the house she had thought feverishly that if he were there, she would rush against him, and even though she couldn't speak to him, she would hold him somehow or other and strike with whatever words came into her mind.

But she had lunch to prepare and autumn kimonos to finish for the children. She mechanically went about these daily tasks, and eventually her wish to attack her husband subsided. How often she had challenged him violently! She was even prepared to crack her head against a stone wall if necessary, but when she attacked him, instead of the stone wall of resistance she expected, she found, to her surprise, a curtain that destroyed her energy. She would listen to her husband's sly reasoning stated with confidence, and then she would lose her resolution in spite of feeling that she hadn't been persuaded by him in the least. If she attacked him at such a time, she couldn't be certain that her first try would be successful.

She ate lunch with her children, settled a quarrel between them, sewed their clothes, prepared supper, gave them a bath, took one herself, and ate her dinner next to the burning mosquito smudge. After they had eaten, the children played themselves into tiredness outdoors. The maid finished her duties in the kitchen, laid out the beds, each in its appointed place, and hung the mosquito net. Otsune sent the children in to wash their hands and then to bed, spread a fly net over her husband's supper on his small table, and put a kettle on the fire in the charcoal brazier in the room next to the bedroom. This was the procedure she followed when Suezo did not return at night.

She had done all these tasks mechanically, and then taking a fan, got under the net and sat on her bed. Suddenly she imagined Suezo in the house of the woman. "I can't sit here," she said to herself. "But what can I do?"

Somehow at the center of her confusion she felt that she ought to walk to Muenzaka. Once when she had bought some beancakes for the children, she had passed the house which Suezo had described as next to the sewing teacher's. She could identify it by its lattice door, the house that woman lived in. All she wanted was to see it. Would there be a light? Would she hear them whispering? If only she could know just that much! But no, she couldn't. In order to get out of her own house she would have to pass the maid's room along the corridor, and at this time of the year the paper sliding doors were removed. She was certain the maid was awake sewing.

"Where you going so late?" Matsu would ask her.

And what could she answer? She might say: "I'm just running out to buy something."

But Matsu would reply: "Certainly not! Let *me* go!"

No matter what Otsune wanted to do, she could not leave the house secretly. "Ah, what can I do?" she thought.

When she had returned home, she had wanted to go to her husband immediately, but what would she have said? She knew her own limitations, and her words would have been meaningless. And then her husband would have invented some tale to trick her and would have succeeded. "I'm not his match in a quarrel. He's too shrewd." She wondered if she weren't better off to keep quiet. But then what would the result have been? "He'd still have his Muenzaka whore, and he'd have no use for me!" What could she do? What?

Again and again her thoughts returned to the point from which they had started. She felt muddled, and she was unable to separate one from the next. Yet somehow she realized that it would be useless to attack Suezo with violence, and she decided to give up that approach at least.

Suddenly her husband entered their room. Otsune intentionally picked up her round fan and, toying with its handle, remained silent.

"Oh?" said Suezo. "Strange looks again? What's wrong?" He was in such good humor that he wasn't in the least offended by his wife's failure to greet him as she usually did.

She still refused to speak. She had meant to avoid any sort of collision, yet upon seeing him she was so annoyed that it was almost impossible to keep herself from assailing him.

"Don't tell me you're worrying about nothing again? Forget it," he said, repeating the last words and putting his hand on his wife's shoulder. He shook her two or three times and then sat down on his bed.

"I'm thinking," she said, "about the future, about what to do with myself. I don't have a family to go back to, and I've got children too."

"What's that? Thinking about what to do with yourself? You don't have to do anything. The world's perfect as it is."

"Go on. You can speak in such a happy-go-lucky way because it's all the better for you if I become something else."

"You're really talking nonsense. That you should become something else? There's no need to change at all. Stay as you are!"

"Go ahead and mock me. You don't have to have anything more to do with me because you don't care if I'm here or not. No, that's wrong. I should have said that what you want is not having me around."

"You're all mixed up. Do you honestly mean that it'd

be better for me if you weren't here? Just the opposite! I couldn't do without you. I need you for a number of things, not the least of which is to look after the children."

"Oh? A prettier mother will take my place and look after them. Though they'd be stepchildren."

"You're really confusing me. We're their parents. They can never be that."

"Are you sure? Do you really believe that? What an egotist you are! Do you mean then to have everything just as it is?"

"Of course."

"Oh? Letting pretty and plain have the same parasols?"

"What did you say? Now what are you up to? Are you telling me the plot of a farce?"

"Yes. I'm not allowed to have a part in a serious play."

"Can't you talk about something more serious than a play? What do you mean by parasols?"

"You know what I mean."

"How can I? I haven't any idea about them."

"I'll tell you then. Do you remember when you bought me a parasol from Yokohama?"

"What about it?"

"You didn't buy it only for me."

"If I didn't, then who else did I buy it for?"

"No, that's not exactly what I mean, I suppose. You did buy it for me, isn't that right? Because the idea just occurred to you when you picked one out for the woman at Muenzaka."

Otsune had injected the subject of the parasols into their discussion, and now that the words had taken definite shape, she couldn't help remembering her earlier rage.

Suezo was startled by this direct hit from his wife, and he almost said aloud: "She's getting closer!" But he was able to look astonished and said: "Impossible! Do you

[handwritten marginal note: social commentary on gender roles]

69

mean, actually mean that—that the same parasol I bought for you is owned by Yoshida's woman?"

"Why not? Since you bought her the very same kind!" she said, her voice suddenly turning into a shriek.

"Is that the only thing you're getting excited about? What an idiot you are! Look. I'm warning you—don't carry your silliness too far. When I bought that parasol for you, they told me it had just come in as a sample. I'm certain of that. But the same kind must easily be available on the Ginza by now and in the neighborhood. I assure you that this case is the same as the play with the theme of the innocent man who was found guilty. Tell me, Otsune, have you met Yoshida's mistress? I don't see how you could have identified her."

"Nothing's easier than that. Everyone in the neighborhood knows her because she's such a *pearl!*"

Otsune's hatred was bound up in her words. Before this she had let him take advantage of her with his lying, but now, as though she were vividly seeing the affair acted out in front of her eyes, nothing could make her feel that her husband's words were convincing enough.

All the while Suezo had been wondering how his wife had met his mistress and if they had spoken to each other, but he thought it would look bad for him at present if he asked Otsune any of the details.

"A *pearl* do you call her? Is that the kind of woman you call a pearl? I would think her face was too flat."

Otsune said nothing about this reply, but the fault Suezo had found with the face of the hated woman appeased her somewhat.

During the night a conciliation again took place after the heated argument, but in Otsune's heart was the pain of a thorn not yet pulled out of flesh.

CHAPTER FIFTEEN

THE ATMOSPHERE in Suezo's house was gradually becoming more and more gloomy. Otsune was often seen gazing absent-mindedly into space and neglecting her work. At such times she paid no attention to the children and scolded them if they bothered her. But then she suddenly realized what she had done and said to them: "I'm sorry. What was it you wanted?" And later she would cry alone.

When the maid said: "What shall I prepare today?" Otsune often failed to answer. Or she might say: "Oh? Anything, anything you wish."

Suezo's children were shunned by their classmates, who sometimes shouted at them: "Moneylenders! Moneylenders!" At Suezo's insistence Otsune had kept them unusually neat. But now they were seen playing in the streets with their hair full of dust and their clothing torn.

The maid went about grumbling at the carelessness of her mistress, and, like a horse that dawdles along the road with an unskilled rider on its back, also became negligent of her own duties so that the fish rotted in the cupboard and the vegetables dried up.

With his passion for order, Suezo found the slovenly state of his home painful. But he couldn't complain because he knew that the cause and the fault were his own. He had prided himself on his ability to correct others by alluding to their weaknesses in a lighthearted manner, but he found that his wife became even more violent when he tried to humor her.

He began to observe her secretly, and he was surprised to find that her strange behavior was more noticeable when he stayed at home, for when he was out of the house she seemed like a person who had awakened from a stupor, and she went about her household tasks. When he learned this fact after talking with the children and the maid, he was at first startled. With his shrewdness in

71

logic he tried to account for her conduct. Her illness, he reasoned, grew worse in his presence because she was dissatisfied with his behavior. He had tried not to act like a cold-hearted husband, and he had avoided any possibility of giving her the impression that there was any estrangement between them. But since he noticed that she was even more out of sorts when he purposely stayed at home, it seemed that his remedy only aggravated her illness. "I'll change my methods," he said to himself.

He began to leave earlier and return later than usual. But the results were worse. The first time he went away earlier, his wife merely looked up in surprise, but when he came back late, instead of giving him a moody glance, she marched upon him with "What you been doing out this long!" Her behavior suggested that she was no longer able to put up with the situation, that she had reached the limits of patience and suffering. And then she burst out crying.

From that time on, whenever he wanted to leave before the usual hour, she tried to stop him with force, saying: "Why so early?"

And when he began to explain, she said: "You're lying!"

But when he started outdoors in spite of her protests, she pleaded: "Wait! Don't go yet! There's something I must ask you!" She would keep him there by holding on to his clothes or by standing in front of the door and refusing to let him pass. She did this even in the presence of the maid. ⁊transgresses against social expectations

Usually Suezo would pass over anything unpleasant by joking about it in order not to make a great issue of a point, but sometimes the maid saw an ugly scene in which he shook off his clinging wife and she fell. But if Suezo said: "All right, I won't go. Tell me what you have to say," his wife would submit a series of difficult problems by no means solvable in a day.

72

"What," she would say, "do you want me to become?"

Sometimes she said: "The way things are, what will my future be?"

In short, Suezo's experiment of an early departure and a late return was totally ineffective in curing his wife of her illness.

He went about the problem in a different way. He realized that when he stayed at home his wife was worse. With this fact in mind he had attempted to be away, but then she had tried to force him to remain. This meant that she was deliberately making herself ill by deliberately keeping him at home. The situation reminded him of an experience he had had when the university medical school was still at Izumibashi.

A student, one Ikai, had borrowed money from him. The boy would pretend he was unconscious of his own appearance, wearing a pair of high clogs on his naked feet and striding with his left shoulder two or three inches higher than the other. Ikai had put off paying Suezo back, had even refused to rewrite his bond, and somehow had always evaded Suezo's pursuit.

One day at the corner of an alley Suezo had come upon him and asked: "Where are you running to?"

"Oh? Why—just over to the jujitsu master's across the way. I say—about that business of yours. You can expect me one of these days." And with that Ikai slipped away.

Suezo pretended to continue on ahead, but he secretly came back, stood at the corner, and spied on the boy. He saw him enter a high-class restaurant.

Suezo hurried through his business, and a short time later he dared to enter the restaurant, saying: "Where's that student Ikai?"

As you might have expected, Ikai was quite surprised to find Suezo there, but assuming his characteristic pose as a hero, called out: "Come into the room, Suezo! I've got a few geishas!" And then forcing the usurer to have some saké, he said: "Don't talk about business here. Just drink at my expense."

This had been Suezo's first experience with geishas, and he couldn't help thinking that one of them, Oshun by name, was quite a filly. She had been drinking too much and, sitting before Ikai, had begun to denounce him for some reason or other.   Suezo hadn't forgotten her words: "Ikai-san, you want us to believe you're brave, the way you put on those grand airs of yours! But you're really nothing but a coward! Let me tell you something for your own benefit. A woman never loves a man who's not kind enough to hit her occasionally. Try to remember that!"

Suezo thought that this might be true not only of geishas but of women in general. Lately his own wife had tried to keep him near her with sulky looks and resistance. This meant that she wanted him to do something to her. "She wants me to hit her!" he said to himself. "Yes, that's it. To really strike her!"

He had forced her to work like an animal without giving her enough food, and, with her feminine qualities held back, she had been transformed into a kind of beast. But since she had moved into a new house and had acquired a servant to help her and to call her *okusan*, she had been raised to a human level and had actually become an ordinary woman. And now she wanted to be beaten like that geisha Oshun.

But what about him? He had pushed his own way through the world with a determination to make a fortune, and cared nothing about what others said of him. He had bowed before fledglings and called them master. It had been his principle that being kicked and trampled didn't matter as long as he made money. And for most of his life, no matter what place he was in or what person came to him, he had prostrated himself as flat as a spider. From what he had seen and learned of the men he had associated with, those who were very considerate of their

74

superiors bullied the people below them and, when they were drunk, even struck their wives and children. But with him no one was higher or lower. He would have thrown himself at any man's feet if it had made him wealthier. Otherwise he had no use for such a person. He would have nothing to do with him, would ignore him. He wouldn't even take the trouble to lift his hand against him. He would rather think about his interest than waste his energies that way. He had treated his wife similarly.

Otsune wanted him to attack her. "Too bad for her, but she won't get that from me." If his debtors had been lemons, he would have squeezed them to the last drop of bitter juice, but he would fight no one.

These were Suezo's latest thoughts on the subject.

CHAPTER SIXTEEN

More and more people passed along Muenzaka. It was September, and the beginning of the term at the university saw the students returning from their homes to their lodgings.

The mornings were as cool as the nights, but the days were still hot. In Otama's house the bamboo blinds were still drawn, their unfaded green covering the window from top to bottom. Otama sat inside with nothing to do. She leaned against a post hung with fans and vacantly looked into the street. After three o'clock the students would pass in small groups. And she knew that whenever they came, the voices of the girls next door would rise like the sounds of so many young sparrows. And attracted by the noise, she would also glance out.

At that time most of the university students were of the type who were later to be called "henchmen." If there were a few gentlemen among them, they were about to graduate. Those who were fair and handsome were mostly unattractive to her, for they seemed shallow and conceited. And those who were not superficial and vain, even the bright students among them, were not preferable because from a woman's point of view they appeared too rough-mannered. Nevertheless, every afternoon Otama, without any particular interest, would look at the students walking past her window.

But one day she was startled by an awareness of something sprouting inside her. This embryo within her imagination had been conceived under the threshold of consciousness and, suddenly taking definite shape, had sprung out.

Her aim in life had been her father's happiness, so she had become a mistress, almost forcibly persuading the old man to accept. She knew she had degraded herself to the lowest limits, yet she had still sought a kind of spiritual comfort in the unselfishness of her choice. But when the person who supported her turned out to be a usurer, she did not know how to cope with this new source of misfortune. The thought tormented her, and she was unable to remove it. She had gone to her father to tell him about it and to ask him to share her pain. But when she had visited him and had seen him living comfortably for the first time, she didn't want to pour a drop of poison into the saké cup he held in his hand. Whatever pain the decision might cost her, she was determined to keep her sadness to herself. And when she had made this decision, the girl, who had always depended on others, had felt for the first time her own independence.

After that, she secretly began to watch what she said and did, and when Suezo came, she started to serve him self-consciously instead of accepting him frankly and sincerely as she had previously done. She would be with him in the room, but her real self was detached, watching the scene from the side. And there it would deride first Suezo and then the other Otama for being under his control. When she first became aware of this condition, she was shocked. But in time she accepted it, and she said to herself: "That's the way you should feel."

Her treatment of Suezo became more cordial but her heart more remote. She came to feel that he did not deserve her gratitude for the protection he gave her, nor could she feel obligated to him for what he did. She did not even feel sorry for him because of her indifference. Conversely, in spite of the fact that she had no accomplishment she could boast of, she couldn't help thinking: "Ah, to be only a usurer's possession all my life."

And watching the students in their walks along the street, she began to speculate: "Isn't there a hero out there? I'll be rescued!"

But when she suddenly found herself indulging in such fancies, she was startled.

— end digression, continue w/ Okada narrative

It was at this point that Okada got to know her. She saw him as just another student who walked past her window, yet when she realized that even though he was eminently handsome, he didn't seem to be conceited, she suspected that there was something about him that made her feel tender toward him. She began to watch for him to pass in the street.

She didn't even know his name or address, but since they exchanged glances so often, she began to have a natural and familiar feeling toward the young man. Once, before she had realized what she was doing, she had even smiled at him, an act of the sort that eludes suppression at the moment when thought is relaxed and restraint paralyzed. She was not the kind of person who had any conscious intention of making him her lover.

When Okada took off his cap and greeted her for the first time, her heart seemed to lift, and she felt herself blushing. A woman has a keen intuition. And Otama clearly knew that Okada's action was done on impulse and not deliberately. She was pleased by this new phase of their friendship, which was casual and quiet and had the window as a sort of boundary. And she pictured to herself again and again the image of Okada at the moment he had bowed.

A mistress who resides in her keeper's home can have the usual protections, but one who lives by herself has troubles she alone knows about.

One day a man in a *happi* coat—a fellow about thirty years old—came to Otama's house and said: "I need some money. I've got to travel, but I can't walk with this wound on my foot."

Otama sent Ume out with a ten-sen piece wrapped in paper. The man opened the wrapper on the spot. "Ten sen? Is that all? It's a mistake!" And he tossed the coin back to her.

Ume was embarrassed, but picked it up and went back in, only to find the man rudely following her and taking a seat opposite Otama, who had been putting some charcoal into the fire. He talked incoherently at great length, bragging at first about having been in prison and then making sentimental complaints. Otama could smell saké on his breath.

She was afraid, yet she held back her tears. Under his eyes, she wrapped in a piece of paper two fifty-sen card-like green notes current at that time and gave them to him. She found that he was more easily satisfied than she she had hoped.

"They're halves, but two'll do. You're pretty clever. And you'll do all right in your life—you will." And with these words he swaggered out with faltering steps.

The incident made Otama feel helpless, and she learned

to "buy" her neighbors. She would prepare a special dish and send it over to the sewing teacher, who lived alone.

Her name was Otei, and she was a matron over forty with a fair complexion. She still looked young, though it was difficult to say just why.

"Until I was thirty," she had told Otama, "I was a high-class servant at a marquis's. But I married and then lost my husband soon after." She spoke elegantly and boasted of her ability to write characters.

"Can you teach me how to write?" Otama had asked. So the woman lent her some copybooks.

One morning Otei came to the back door to thank Otama for what she had sent over the day before. In the course of their talk while Otei stood at the door, the woman said to Otama: "I believe you know Okada-san, isn't that so?"

Otama had never heard the name before, yet it flashed through her mind that the sewing teacher had referred to the student, that she had seen Okada greeting her, and that the situation compelled her to pretend she knew him. After a brief hesitation that was not perceptible to the other woman, Otama readily answered: "Yes, I do."

"He's handsome all right," said Otei, "and yet, I hear there's not a flaw in his conduct."

"You seem to know him well," said Otama boldly.

"Madame Kamijo tells me that none of the students at her lodging can match him." And with these words Otei returned to her house.

Otama felt as though she herself had been praised and repeated to herself: "Kamijo! Okada!"

CHAPTER SEVENTEEN

WITH THE passing of time Suezo's visits to Otama grew even more frequent, for not only did he come without fail at night as he had previously done, but he began to visit at irregular periods during the day as well. These were moments of escape from his wife, who followed him about with the annoying demand: "You've got to do something for me!"

When he tried to persuade her that nothing had to be done and that it was all right to live as they had been living, she insisted: "I can't go on like this! I can't return to my parents' home! I can't give up my children! I'm getting old!" These were the objections she listed to any possible change in her life.

Suezo often repeated: "There's no need to make any change. We'll stay as we are."

And as they argued about these matters, Otsune would lose her temper and get so wrought up that Suezo would rush out of the house. He had always been able to reason logically and mathematically, so his wife's words were ridiculous and unintelligible to him. She seemed to him like a person struggling to find his way out of a room that has three walls and a door wide open behind him. All one could possibly say to such a creature was "Turn around!"

Her life was more comfortable than it had ever been, and she was neither oppressed nor restrained. True, the Muenzaka woman was a new factor for her, but Suezo had grown neither more cold nor more cruel because of the woman—examples to the contrary can certainly be found among other men—and he told himself: "I'm even kinder, more generous." Why, he wondered, didn't she see the door, still left wide open?

Of course there was a certain amount of selfishness in Suezo's thought, for even though Otsune was receiving more material comfort than she had in the past and her

she is more secure, physically but not emotionally

husband's words and attitude had not altered, it was unreasonable for him to expect his wife to think in the same way she had thought when Otama hadn't existed. Wasn't the woman a splinter in Otsune's eye? And didn't he have the slightest intention of pulling it out and giving his wife relief? Otsune was unable to think rationally and couldn't follow an argument; thus the door Suezo thought open was not so to her. In fact, a heavy shadow fell across the doorway where she had hoped to get a glimpse of ease for the present and hope for the future.

One morning after a quarrel Suezo rushed out of the house. It was probably a few minutes past ten-thirty. He thought he would go directly to Muenzaka, but when he saw the maid and his children heading that way, he turned in another direction and hurried ahead aimlessly. Occasionally he muttered some foul words to himself.

As he reached Shohei-bashi, he saw a geisha coming from the opposite direction. He first imagined that she looked like Otama, but as he passed her he saw that her face was freckled. "My Otama's more beautiful," he thought. He was aware of an immediate sense of satisfaction, and stopping on the bridge, he watched the geisha's departure. Speculating that she was out shopping, he saw her disappear into an alley.

The Megane-bashi was a new bridge at that time, and Suezo walked along towards Yanagihara after crossing it. Suddenly he saw a man and a girl of twelve or thirteen at their customary places under a large parasol that had been planted in the soil by a willow tree near the river. The girl was doing a folk dance, and, as usual, a number of spectators were there. When Suezo stopped for a few minutes to watch, a man almost ran into him. Suezo's eyes detected the stranger quickly, and as Suezo turned back and met his gaze, the pickpocket hurried away. "What professional stupidity!" Suezo muttered to himself, at the same time feeling under his kimono to see if his wallet were still safe. The thief must have been an ignorant fellow, for when Suezo had had a quarrel with his wife, his nerves were so tense that he noticed things he wouldn't usually have seen. His natural sensitiveness was made the keener, so that a pickpocket could hardly conceive of robbing him before Suezo sensed his intention. But on such occasions his power of controlling himself—in which he took great pride—was lax to a slight degree, though so slight that ordinary people would not have noticed. A very sensitive observer might have discovered that Suezo was a little more talkative than usual and that there was something restless and unnatural about him as he spoke and behaved in an officiously kind manner.

Suezo thought he had been out for quite some time, but when he glanced at his watch as he continued along the edge of the river, it was eleven, only a half hour since his departure, perhaps less.

Though he didn't know where to go, he seemed, as he passed along, like a person on an important business trip. A short distance before the turn at Imagawa Lane, he saw a house advertising "Rice-in-Tea." Inside, he could buy a tray of a few dishes with pickles and tea for only twenty sen. "I've a mind to go in," he thought, but since it was too early for lunch, he went on, turned right, and came into the broad street leading to Manaita-bashi.

Crossing, he noticed on the right side a shop dealing in various kinds of pet birds whose lively cries attracted the passersby. He stopped in front of the shop—you can still see it today—and looked up at the cages of parrots and parakeets hung high on the eaves, while on the floor he could see those of white doves and Korean pigeons. His glance moved to the cages of small song birds piled up row after row at the back of the shop. These little birds sang the loudest and flew about in the liveliest fashion. Among them the greatest in number and the noisiest in their singing were the light-yellow imported canaries. And as his eye brushed past them, he was attracted to the linnets, which sat quietly in their vivid colors. It suddenly occurred to him to buy a pair for Otama. "She could feed them. How charming to see her with them!" he thought.

Suezo asked the price, and, although the old shopkeeper seemed indifferent to making a sale, bought a brace of linnets. After he had paid for them, the shopkeeper asked: "How will you carry them?"

"Don't they come with a cage?"

"Of course not."

Suezo almost had to beg the man to make another sale. The old man put his withered hand roughly into the cage and, catching two of the linnets, transferred them to an empty cage.

"Can you tell if they're male and female?" Suezo asked.

"I should think so," said the old man reluctantly.

As Suezo retraced his steps, he carried the cage with the two linnets. His pace was unhurried then, and every so often he would lift the cage and look inside. The mood in which he had fled his house seemed to have been wiped away, and the tender feeling usually hidden inside him came to the surface. Perhaps frightened by the swaying of the cage, the birds, sitting motionless with their wings folded, clung tightly to the perch.

Each time Suezo looked at them, he felt as though he wanted to hurry off to Muenzaka to hang the cage in Otama's window.

But coming along Imagawa Lane, he stopped at the house of "Rice-in-Tea" for lunch. He put the cage behind the tray the waitress brought him and looked at the pretty birds. And thinking all the while of Otama, he ate the rather inferior meal with gusto.

CHAPTER EIGHTEEN

SUEZO's gift of the linnets to Otama provided the opportunity for Otama and Okada to speak to each other.

Their relationship reminds me of the weather of that autumn. At that time my father, who is now dead, had planted fall flowers in the garden behind his house, and one Sunday after returning from the Kamijo, I saw him tying stalks of flowers and agueweeds along with other types of plants to props of thin bamboo canes set in the ground, for a typhoon was expected September first, the so-called Two Hundred and Tenth Day. But the twenty-four hours passed calmly. Next we thought the Two Hundred and Twentieth Day would be the dreaded one, but it wasn't. For several days after that, restless and threatening clouds were seen. Sometimes it was so hot that people thought summer had come again. The southeast wind seemed to gather strength but died away. "Two Hundred and Tenth Day," said my father, "is being paid off in installments."

When I returned to the Kamijo from my home one Sunday evening, none of the students were in, and everything was quiet. I had gone to my room to relax, when I suddenly heard a match struck in the next room.

I wanted company, so I called out: "Is that you, Okada?"

I could hardly catch his reply. I had become friendly with him, and we had avoided all the polite formalities, but his answer struck me as odd.

I thought that he had been daydreaming. "Do you mind if I come in?" I asked, curious to see what was wrong.

"That's what I was hoping. I came back quite a while ago, and I've done nothing since. When I heard you, I was aroused and thought I'd light my lamp." This time he answered me in a clear voice.

I went into the corridor and opened the sliding doors to my friend's room. He was sitting with his elbows on his desk and was looking into the outside gloom through his open window, which directly faced the Iron Gate.

Okada turned to me, saying: "It's unusually sultry, isn't it? And with these two or three mosquitoes in my room. . . . Annoying pests!"

I went to the side of his desk and sat there informally, saying: "My father calls it paying for Two Hundred and Tenth in installments."

"What? Oh. That's an interesting way of putting it. Well, maybe he's right. The weather was so unsettled— first clouding and then clearing—that I couldn't decide whether to go out or stay in. So I spent all morning just lying here and reading the *Kimpeibai* you lent me. I got to the point where I couldn't think straight, so I went out for a walk after lunch. And something strange happened."

He said all this without looking at me. Instead he stared out the window.

"What was it?"

"I killed a snake," he said, turning toward me.

"And rescued a beauty, eh?"

"No, only a bird. But it had something to do with a beauty."

"Now this interests me! What's it about?"

CHAPTER NINETEEN

Another shift in narrative structure

THIS IS what Okada told me.

That afternoon the clouds moved quickly, and sporadic gusts of wind blew up the dust on the roads and then subsided. Okada's reading of his Chinese novel had given him a headache. He had gone out for some air and from habit had turned toward Muenzaka. He felt dizzy. In old Chinese novels, especially in the *Kimpeibai*, usually after every ten or twenty pages of innocent description, the author invariably throws in an indecent scene as if he were quite punctually fulfilling a promise.

"I must have looked awfully silly after reading that sort of book," said Okada.

When he came to the stone wall of Iwasaki's mansion on the right where the slope begins to descend, he saw a group of people on the left. They stood in front of the house he always looked at in passing. This was the only fact that Okada didn't tell me at that time. There were about ten women present, and more than half of them were young girls talking as noisily as a group of singing birds. Okada couldn't see anything, and without any particular curiosity he turned toward them and took two or three steps from the middle of the road.

The women were looking at a single point, and as he followed their glance, he discovered the cause of the confusion: a bird cage hung in the window of the house. No wonder the women were upset. When Okada saw the cage, he too was startled. A bird was rushing about inside, flapping its wings and shrieking. And looking more closely, Okada noticed a large snake with its head through the bars frightening the bird. The snake had wedged its way between two thin bamboo sticks without actually breaking the cage. But by forcing itself through, it had widened the gap between the bars as wide as its body.

Okada took a few steps forward to get a better view, and as a result he stood just behind the row of girls.

As if by common consent, the girls seemed relieved to have found a rescuer in him; they made room for him and pushed him forward, whereupon Okada discovered a new fact: the bird had not been alone.

The mate to the one fluttering about was trapped in the snake's mouth. And though only one of its wings was caught, it seemed to be dead, perhaps from fear, for its other wing drooped and its body looked like a piece of cotton.

At that moment a woman who was somewhat older than the rest and was apparently the mistress of the house said hurriedly to Okada, yet with modesty: "Can't you help? That awful snake!" And she added: "These girls from next door just came out, but it's beyond a woman's ability!"

"This lady here," one of the girls said, "heard the birds making noise, so she opened the sliding windows. We heard her scream when she saw the snake. So we dropped our work and ran over. But we can't do anything. And our teacher's stepped out for a moment. But even if she were here now, she couldn't help. She's too old." The sewing teacher took her holiday on every fifth day of the month instead of on Sunday. That was why the girls had come that day.

When Okada was telling me this, he said: "The woman was quite beautiful." But he didn't say that he had seen her before and that he had greeted her each time he passed her house.

Without answering, Okada stood under the cage and examined how the snake had got there. It had crawled up to the cage hanging in the window by approaching it from under the eaves between Otama's house and the house of the sewing teacher. Its body lay on a crossarm of the eave like a rope thrown over the support, and its tail was hidden around a post at the corner of the house. The snake was quite long. Probably, Okada thought, it had come from the thick growth of trees and grass on the estate across the street. And what with the strange weather, it had strayed out and come upon the birds.

Okada was temporarily confused by the situation. It was obvious that the women couldn't do anything.

"Do you have something sharp in the house?" he asked.

87

"Run in," said the mistress to a small girl, "and get a knife from the kitchen." Perhaps the girl was the maid, for even though she wore a summer kimono similar to the other girls', she had tucked up her sleeves with a purple sash.

The girl frowned as if to say: "I don't like the fish knife used for cutting snakes!" *the snake will poison the knife*

"Don't worry," her mistress said, "I'll buy you a new one."

This satisfied the girl, and she ran in and quickly brought out the knife.

Okada took it from her impatiently, and letting his wooden clogs slip from his feet, he easily set one foot on the window sill; with gymnastic skill his left hand was already grasping the crossarm of the eave.

Okada knew that even though the knife was new it wasn't sharp, so he had no intention of cutting the snake in two at one blow. Pushing the snake's body against the beam with the knife, Okada moved the blade up and down a few times. He felt as though he were breaking glass as the scales of the body were pierced.

By this time the head of the bird had already been sucked into the snake's mouth, and when the snake felt itself being wounded, its body began writhing like the rise and fall of a wave. Yet it refused to disgorge its victim or to pull itself out of the cage. *Suezo refused to admit his lies*

After Okada had pushed and pulled the knife back and forth several times, the dull edge finally divided the snake in two like a chunk of meat on a chopping board. The lower part of its body, which had been in continual movement, first fell down with a thud on the beard grass just below the roof. But the other half, tumbling off the beam on which it had rested, dangled in the air, the head still stuck in the cage. The head had doubled in size because half the bird remained in the snake's mouth, and the bamboo bars, bent like bows, continued to hold it in place. The weight of the dead body inclined the cage about forty-five degrees. The surviving bird kept up its mad dance, its wings fluttering with an energy that was still wonderfully unexhausted.

Okada withdrew his hand from the supporting cross-arm and jumped to the ground. At this point a few of the girls, who had watched breathlessly all the while, returned to the sewing teacher's house.

"We've got to take down the cage and pull out the snake's head," said Okada, looking at the mistress.

But neither she nor her maid had heart enough to go in to lower the linen string that kept the cage suspended, for the severed end of the dangling snake was bleeding on the window sill.

Just then a madcap voice said: "Should I take it down?"

Everyone turned to the speaker, the errand-boy of a saké dealer. He was the only one who had come along on this dreary Sunday afternoon while Okada was killing the snake. Holding a saké bottle bound with a rope in one hand and his account book in the other, the boy had stood there as an idle spectator. But when the lower portion of the snake landed on the grass, he had abandoned his bottle and book on the ground, and picking up a small stone, he had struck the raw flesh of the snake, every blow to the writhing body giving him much pleasure. *he enjoys violence and harming others*

"I hate troubling you, but please do it for us," said the mistress politely. The maid took the boy inside, and soon he reappeared at the window, climbed on the board with the flowerpot on it, and stretching himself as far as he could, barely managed to reach the string with his outstretched arms.

"Do you want it?" he asked the maid, but when she shrank from the cage, he jumped off the window sill and carried it through the house out to the entrance.

"I'm holding the cage, so you've got to wipe up the blood," the boy said. "It's on the mats too!" he proudly advised the girl, who followed him out.

"Oh yes! Do that right away!" said her mistress, and the maid hurried back in.

Okada looked into the cage and saw the bird trembling on the perch. More than half of its mate's body was lost in the snake's mouth. Even as Okada had cut the snake apart, it had tried up to the last moment to swallow its victim.

"Do you want me to get the snake out?" the boy asked, turning to Okada.

"Think you can?" Okada said with a smile. "All right, but lift it to the middle of the bars first or else you'll break them."

The boy was successful, and pulling at the tail of the bird with his fingertips, he said: "Why! Even though it's dead, the devil won't let go!"

Thinking there was nothing further to see, the remaining pupils of the sewing teacher went inside.

"Well," said Okada, looking around, "I'd better go too."

Apparently lost in thought, the mistress suddenly turned to him on hearing his words. She tried to speak, but was forced to hesitate and turned her eyes away. At that moment she noticed a spot of blood on Okada's hand.

"Ah!" she cried. "You've stained your hand." And calling her girl, she had a wooden wash basin brought to the entrance.

When Okada told me the story, he did not give me a detailed account of the woman's attitude, but he said to me: "I don't know how she could have found a small stain of blood on my little finger."

While Okada was washing his hands, the errand boy, who had been attempting to pull the dead bird from the snake's throat, cried out: "Hey!"

The mistress of the house was standing beside Okada with a new towel folded in her hand, and hearing the boy's cry, she asked: "What's wrong?"

"The other bird nearly flew out the hole the snake made!" said the lad, putting his open hands on the cage.

"Keep your hand there," said Okada, wiping his fingers on the towel she had given him. Turning to her, he asked: "Do you have a piece of strong thread? We can tie up the damaged part of the cage and keep that other bird from flying out."

"Will a paper cord for tying hair do?" the mistress asked, after a moment's thought.

"All right," said Okada.

"Get it from the mirror stand," the woman said to her maid. When the girl came out, Okada took the cord from her and in a haphazard crisscross fashion tied up the opening left by the bent bars.

"Well," said Okada, going out the entrance, "I guess there's nothing more for me to do."

"I'm . . . then thank you," said the woman, unable to express herself as she followed him outside.

Turning to the boy, Okada said: "Since you've done so much already, how about throwing the snake away somewhere?"

"All right. I'll throw it in the deep part of the ditch at the bottom of the slope. Do you have a piece of rope?" he asked, looking around.

"I have some. Wait a minute please," said the mistress, whispering to her maid.

"Goodbye then," said Okada. And he went down the slope without turning his head.

Okada had gone this far, and facing me, he said: "You see, I exerted myself too much even for a beauty."

"I think you did," I said. But I added quite frankly: "Killing a snake for a beautiful woman is an interesting story. It's almost like a fairy tale. But it doesn't seem to me that your story's finished."

"What? Don't be foolish. If it weren't, do you think I'd have published it?"

I think he spoke without affectation, yet if it really ended there, I felt that he was sorry it did.

I had said that his story was similar to a fairy tale, but another idea occurred to me as I listened to him. But I didn't tell him this. It seemed to me that Okada, who had been reading the *Kimpeibai*, had met a woman like Kinren, the heroine of that novel.

All the students at the university, including those who never borrowed from Suezo, knew the usurer, the money-lender who had risen from the position of a school serv-ant. But there were some who didn't know that the woman at Muenzaka was his mistress. Okada was among these. At that time I hadn't learned any of the details about her, yet I did know that the woman living next to the sewing teacher was Suezo's mistress.

In this instance I knew a little more than my friend.

fragmented narratives run parallel to one another

CHAPTER TWENTY

narrative shift

ON THE day that Okada killed the snake, a sudden change took place in Otama after she had spoken to him, for up to that time they had only looked at one another.

A woman may have her heart set on a particular article, yet she may not go so far as to think of buying it. Each time she passes it, she may stop and look into the window where the article, say a ring or a watch, is on display. She doesn't go to that shop deliberately, but whenever she happens to be in the neighborhood on some business or other, she always makes it a point to examine it. Though she recognizes that she will never be able to buy the article, the renunciation and the desire to have it often give rise to a not too keen but rather faint and sweetly sad emotion. And she enjoys feeling it. On the other hand, a particular item she can afford and has determined to buy gives her acute pain. It troubles her so much that she gets restless. Even when she knows she can own it in a few days, she can hardly wait for the moment of possession. Occasionally she will even go out to get it on impulse—this in spite of heat or cold, darkness, rain, or snow. The woman who steals articles in a shop is not carved out of a different wood. But there is a distinction. A shoplifter blurs the line between the expensive items she yearns for and can't buy and articles she can buy if she has the money.

Otama's longing for Okada had been like that of a woman for an expensive article she admired from a distance, but he now turned into an article she wanted to buy.

His rescue of her bird had given her an opportunity for becoming better acquainted with him. Should she send Ume to him with some token of gratitude? And if so, what should it be? Perhaps some bean-jam buns from Fujimura's confectionery? But that would reveal a lack of wit: too commonplace, what anyone else would do. If she avoided the commonplace, say by making him an elbow-cushion sewed out of small pieces of colored cloth, he would smile at it as though it were a token of girlish love. She couldn't think of a good possibility. But supposing she had made a choice, would it be right for Ume to take it to him?

Only a few days ago at a shop on Naka-cho, she had had her name card printed, but only that attached to the gift would not be satisfactory. She wished to write a few lines, but how could she? She had only gone through elementary school, and since she had not had any time to improve her brush work, she couldn't even write a note properly. The sewing teacher had told her she had worked at a lord's house, and if Otama had asked her to write, the sewing teacher would have done so at once. But Otama didn't want that. She had nothing to write that would have made her feel ashamed, yet she didn't want anyone else to know that she had written to Okada. Then what should she do?

In the same way that a route is followed back and forth along the same road, Otama thought this much through in straight order and then in reverse, abandoning the problem while she dressed and gave directions to Ume for the kitchen. But later she speculated about it once more.

And then Suezo arrived. While she poured him some saké, she began to think about the problem again.

"What's on your mind so much?" Suezo asked, reproaching her slightly.

"Why!" she said, smiling meaninglessly but with a hidden fluttering of her heart, "nothing at all."

Lately she had trained herself a great deal in not permitting her sharp-eyed lover to find out what she was concealing from him.

After Suezo had left, she dreamed that she had finally purchased a box of cakes and had rushed Ume out with it. But after the girl had gone, Otama discovered that she hadn't included a name card or a note. And she was startled into wakefulness.

Perhaps Okada had not taken a walk or she had missed him as he passed, for the day after the snake-killing, Otama didn't get a chance to look at the face she wanted so much to see. But the following day he was outside as usual. He glanced toward her window, yet it was so dark inside that he didn't recognize her. And the next day, at the time he usually came by, she took out a broom and swept the interior of the doorway. There was little dust to get rid of, and she occupied herself by placing first to the right and then to the left a pair of wooden clogs.

"Oh, dear!" said Ume, coming out of the kitchen. "Let me do that!"

"Don't trouble about it," said Otama. "You look after the cooking. I'm only doing this because I don't have anything else to do." And with these words the girl was driven back to the kitchen.

At that moment Okada came by with his usual greeting. Red to the ears, Otama stood bolt upright with the broom in her hand, but she let him walk on without saying a word.

She threw down her broom as though it were a pair of tongs that burned her hand, kicked off her sandals, and ran into the house.

Sitting before the charcoal brazier, she toyed with a pair of fire tongs over the kindled coals, thinking to herself: "I'm a fool! I thought that if I stared outside on such a cool day with the window open, it would look strange. So I purposely waited for him outside, pretending the place had to be swept. And yet—yet when he did come, I couldn't say a word! No matter how embarrassed I am in front of Suezo, I can say anything when I have a mind to. But why can't I speak to Okada-san? It's natural for me to thank him for his help. If I can't even give him my thanks, I'll never have the chance to talk to him. I'd be only too glad to send Ume with a gift, but since there's a problem in sending it to him and since I can't say anything to him, what else can I do? Why couldn't I speak just now? Well, yes, yes, I was about to. But I didn't know what to say! Calling his name would have been too familiar a way for me. It would be strange to say to a man who was looking at me: 'Why, good day!' Now that I'm thinking about it, it's no wonder that I was so upset at the time. For even now when I've enough time to think, I don't have the right words. No, it's foolish to think in this way. I didn't have to say anything. All I had to do was run out to him at once. Then he certainly would have stopped. And once he had, I might have said: 'Please, I must thank you for your kindness of the other day.' That or some such thing."

Reasoning in this way and toying with the coals, she was surprised to find the lid of the iron kettle jumping up and down, and she slid it aside to let out the steam.

From that day on, she carried on a personal debate about the two alternatives, namely, to speak to Okada herself or to send Ume to him with a message. Meanwhile, with the days growing cooler in the evening, it would have looked strange to leave the window open. Usually the grounds were swept once in the morning, but after the broom incident Ume swept in the evening as well, leaving Otama no chance to do it herself.

Otama began to go to the public bath at a later hour in order to see Okada on the way, but the distance between her house and the bath at the foot of the slope was too short to give much of an opportunity for such a meeting. On the other hand, as the days advanced, it was becoming more awkward for her to send her maid to him.

She tried to resign herself temporarily by giving her thought a new direction: she hadn't yet thanked Okada. Since she hadn't returned the kindness which she was duty-bound to return, she was under an obligation to him. And it was obvious that he knew she was. It might be all the better for her to remain in that situation instead of trying to repay him in a clumsy way.

Still she wanted to get to know him better by using her obligation to him as a starting point for more contact.

social

Otama is ultimately the main character of the book

96

In fact, she was secretly giving the matter a great deal of thought in order to bring this about.

By nature Otama was a spirited woman, and in the few months since she had become Suezo's mistress, her painful experience of the outward contempt shown a mistress and the inward envy of the people around her enabled her to set the world at naught. Yet since she was basically a good woman and had not yet had too much experience in life, she felt it difficult to visit a university student at his lodginghouse.

There were some fine autumn days when she could keep her window open and exchange a salute with Okada, but their relationship remained unchanged since that memorable event, and no new state of intimacy developed from her having spoken to him once and having handed him a towel. And the situation was more than frustrating for her.

When Suezo came and talked with her over the charcoal brazier, she imagined what it would be like if Okada were there instead. At first, she felt she was being unfaithful, but she gradually came to feel no shame in speaking in tune with Suezo's words while thinking of Okada all the time. Moreover, when she submitted to Suezo, the image of Okada was behind her closed eyes. Sometimes they were together in her dreams. He was there without any troublesome arrangements to be made. But the moment she thought how happy she was, the man turned into Suezo instead of Okada. She would be startled and would awake, her nerves so strained that sometimes she cried out in a fret.

It was already November, and the days settled into Indian summer, so Otama had an excuse for keeping the window open to await Okada's daily walk. Previously a group of chilly and wet days had prevented her from seeing him for several days at a time, and she had become despondent. But she was of so mild a temperament that she didn't give her maid any trouble with unreasonable demands, nor did she give Suezo any sorry looks.

During these periods she would remain alone at the brazier with her elbows resting on its frame. She would sit silently and would seem so lost that one day Ume asked her: "Is anything wrong?"

But now that she could see Okada for many days in a row, she felt buoyant, and one morning she walked to her father's house with a light step.

She visited him without fail once a week, but she never stayed more than an hour. This was because her father refused to let her stay longer. When she called on him, he treated her always with the same kindness. And if he had any good things to serve, he brought them out and made tea for her. But, this finished, he said: "You'd better go now."

He said this not merely because of the impatience of an old man but also because he thought it selfish of him to detain his daughter for long when he had sent her out to do service. On her second or third visit she had informed him that she could stay longer because her master never came in the morning, but the old man wouldn't allow her to take her time.

"Well, it may be true," he had told her, "that as yet he hasn't come in the morning, but you can't be certain when he'll get there on some unexpected business. If you had asked him, and got his permission, it would be all right. But since you've only stopped here on your way from shopping, you shouldn't stay long. You wouldn't have any excuse if he thought you were idling away the time."

She knew her father would be offended if he learned about Suezo's profession, and she worried about this. When she visited him, she wanted to find out if he had discovered anything, but so far he was ignorant of the matter. It was natural that he remained so. Since moving here, he had started to rent books, and with his glasses on, he would sit all day and read. He borrowed histories with a romantic twist and biographies, both kinds of books exclusively printed in a particular script. If the keeper of the library showed him works of fiction and recommended them, the old man would say: "What? Those lies!"

At night, since he tired of reading, he would go to the variety hall where he would listen to the comic tales and hear the dramatic ballads being recited without questioning their truth or falsehood. But unless the teller was a particular favorite of his, he seldom went to the hall at Hirokoji, where the narratives were chiefly historical. These were his only hobbies, and since he never gossiped with outsiders, he didn't make any new friends. Therefore, he had little chance of hearing about Suezo's background.

Nevertheless, some of his neighbors wondered about the fair visitor to the old man's house, and at last they identified her as the usurer's mistress. If the neighbors on both sides of the old man's house had been chatterboxes, the unpleasant report might have somehow reached him in spite of the lack of communication between them. But fortunately they were not likely to disturb his peace of mind, for one of them was a minor clerk at a museum who spent of all his leisure hours collecting model copybooks of Chinese characters and learning how to use the brush, and the other man was an engraver who had remained at the old craft in spite of his fellow-craftsmen's having abandoned the trade in order to make seals. Of the houses in the same row as the old man's, the trading places included only a noodle restaurant, a rice-cake shop, and a store dealing in combs.

Even before the old man heard his daughter's gentle greeting, he was conscious of her visit from the movement of the door and the light step of her clogs. He would put down the book he was reading and wait for her entrance into the room. If he could take off his glasses and look at his precious daughter, it was a festival day for him. Of course he could see better with his glasses on, but it seemed to him that they set up a barrier between him and Otama. Usually he had so much to tell her that after she had gone, he always remembered something or other left unsaid. But he never failed to say: "Give Suezo my greeting."

On that day when Otama had left her house in such a joyous mood, she also found her father in good humor, listened to him recite a court tale, and ate a rice wafer of enormous size. "I bought it," he said, "at a branch shop that just opened at Hirokoji. It's from the famous bakery at O-senju."

He asked her many times during their talk: "Isn't it time to go?"

"Don't worry about it!" Otama said smiling. And she stayed there almost until noon.

She knew that if she had told her father that lately Suezo sometimes came at the most unexpected hours, the old man would have urged her more frequently to go back.

Otama had become more brazen and was not very anxious about Suezo's visits during her absence.

CHAPTER TWENTY-ONE

IT WAS getting colder, and the boards outside the wooden drain from the sink were covered with a thick frost. Otama pitied Ume for having to draw water from the deep well with a long rope, and she bought the girl a pair of gloves. But Ume, who thought it too troublesome for her to put them on and take them off in doing kitchen work, guarded the gloves as a precious gift and still labored at the well with her bare hands. Otama would say: "Use hot water for washing clothes and for wiping the floors." But Ume's hands still got rough and chapped.

Otama said, sympathizing with her: ' The worst thing's to keep your hands wet. Wipe them carefully and dry them each time you take them out of water."

She bought Ume a cake of soap for the purpose. But the girl's hands became rougher, and it pained Otama to see them in that condition. "Why do her hands get so red and cracked?" she wondered to herself. "I did as much work as she does now and mine weren't like that."

Otama had been in the habit of getting out of bed as soon as her eyes opened in the morning, but when Ume would say: "The sink's frozen. Stay where you are," her mistress remained under the covers.

As a safeguard against obscene thoughts, educators warn young people not to remain awake after going to bed and to get up as soon as they awaken, for in the vigors of youth kept warm in bed, an image like the flower of a poisonous plant blooming in fire is apt to be engendered. At such times Otama's imagination was unbridled. Her eyes would glow, and the flush would spread from her eyelids to her cheeks as though she had drunk too much saké.

One frosty morning after a starry night, Otama remained idly in bed for a long time—a habit she had acquired of late. Not until she saw the morning sun through the front window did she rise. And with only a narrow band around her kimono and a housecoat over it, she stood brushing her teeth in the open corridor outside her room. Suddenly the lattice door opened, and Ume's friendly voice greeted a visitor. Otama heard him enter the room.

"Hey there! You lazy-riser!" said Suezo, sitting at the brazier.

"Oh! Excuse me," Otama said, hastily taking the toothbrush from her mouth. "You've come awfully early."

To Suezo's eyes, her smiling face, flushed somewhat as though the blood had rushed to her head, was lovelier than ever. Since coming to live at Muenzaka, she had become prettier by the day. At first Suezo admired the maiden-like naïveté of her manners. But lately they had changed, and he was even more enchanted. He saw this transformation as evidence of her understanding of love, and he was proud that she had learned what it was from him. In spite of his insight into reality, this was a ridiculous misunderstanding of his mistress' state of mind. At first she had served him faithfully, but as a result of her unhappiness and the reflectiveness caused by the sudden changes in her life, she had arrived at a self-consciousness which might almost be called impudent negligence. She had acquired that coolness of mind that most women in the world who do have it can reach only after experiences with many men. Suezo found it stimulating to be trifled with by her coolness. She had begun to neglect her duties with an increasing disregard for them, and she had become less tidy. But this untidiness fanned Suezo's passions to a higher intensity. He did not realize the basis for these alterations, so he was more charmed than before.

Squatting down and drawing a brass basin near her, Otama said: "Turn around, please."

"Why?" he asked, lighting a cigarette.

"Because I'm washing."

"Don't worry about me. Go ahead."

"But if you sit there staring at me, I can't."

"My, but you're proper. How's this? All right?" And with his back toward the corridor Suezo smoked his cigarette. "What an innocent thing she is," he thought.

Pushing back the top of her kimono and letting it slip

off her shoulders, she washed herself quickly. She was not as careful as she usually was, but since she had no blemish to hide or smooth over by using make-up in secret, she had no reason to feel embarrassed at being observed.

Before long, Suezo turned around. While she was washing, she didn't notice that he had turned, but after finishing and drawing the mirror stand in front of her, she saw his face in it, the cigarette still in his mouth.

"Ah? So that's the kind of man you are!" she said, continuing to comb her hair.

A triangular patch of white skin revealing her neck and part of her back could be seen above the loosened kimono, and her soft arms, lifted high and exposed a few inches above the elbows, were sights Suezo never tired of.

"Don't rush," he said, fearing his silence would hurry her and making his tone deliberately easy. "I haven't come for anything in particular. When you asked me the other day when I'd be here, I told you this evening. But I've got to go to Chiba. If everything goes all right, I'll be able to come back tomorrow. If not, maybe the day after."

"Oh?" said Otama, wiping her comb and looking back at him. She made herself seem sad.

"Be a good child and wait for me," said Suezo humorously, putting his cigarette case in his kimono sleeve. Suddenly he got up and went out to the entrance.

Throwing her comb down, Otama said: "Oh, excuse me for not giving you even a cup of tea!" But when she stood up to see him off, he had already opened the door and was gone.

Ume brought Otama's breakfast in from the kitchen and, setting it down, bowed with her hands on the mats to apologize.

"What are you asking pardon for?" said Otama, sitting at the brazier and knocking the ashes off the fire with a pair of charcoal tongs.

"For being late with the tea."

"Oh, is that all? Why, I was only being polite. Your master doesn't mind," she said, taking up her chopsticks.

Watching her eat, Ume thought Otama was unusually good-natured, though for that matter her mistress was seldom in a bad temper. A trace of the smile with which Otama had said "What are you asking pardon for?" still remained on her faintly flushed cheeks. The maid wondered why Otama had smiled, but she was too simple to probe causes. And she felt infected by her mistress's happiness.

Looking at Ume's face and making herself even more cheerful, Otama said: "Ah, don't you want to go home?"

The maid's eyes rounded in wonder. As late as the second decade of the Meiji era, the customs of the tradesmen's houses in Edo were still kept up, although they were slowly dying out. As a result, even those servants whose families lived in the city were not easily allowed to go home except on Servants' Day.

"Well," Otama continued, "since your master's not expected this evening, you might as well go and spend the night with your family if you wish."

"Oh, do you mean it?" Ume did not doubt Otama's sincerity, but she felt that she was unworthy of the favor allowed her.

"Why should I lie? I'd never play tricks on you unfairly. Don't put away the breakfast things, but go on—now! Take all the time you want, and stay there for the night. But don't forget to come back early tomorrow morning."

"Oh, yes—I will!" Ume said, her face flushed with delight. She saw her father's house, his two or three rickshaws in the entrance, her father resting on a cushion placed in a space scarcely wider than the cushion itself between a chest of drawers and the brazier. And, her father at work, Ume also pictured her mother there, her sidelocks hanging loosely over her cheeks, a thin sash holding up her sleeves and seldom taken off her shoulders. These images, like so many silhouettes, came alternately in rapid succession to Ume's mind.

When Otama had finished the meal, Ume took the tray away. The girl felt she should wash the dishes even though she had been told to leave them, and when Otama came in with something folded in a piece of paper, Ume was rinsing the bowls and plates in a small wooden bucket filled with hot water.

"Oh, you're washing them even though I said not to? I'll do it for you. It's not much work for me to wash a few things. You did your hair last night, so it looks all right, don't you think? Hurry and dress. I've nothing to give you as a present for your parents, so take this."

Otama handed Ume the folded paper. Inside was a half-yen note, blue-colored and resembling a playing card.

Otama had hurried Ume off, and like a good maid with her sleeves tied up with a sash and her kimono ends tucked up under her *obi*, she went directly into the kitchen. She began the half-washed bowls and plates as though it were a pleasant pastime for her. She was used to such work and could do it far more quickly and thoroughly than Ume could, but now she went about it more slowly than a child playing with its toys. She cleaned one plate for five minutes. Her face was animated, rosy, her eyes distant.

Hopeful images entered her mind. Women pitiably waver in their decisions until they have made up their minds, yet once they have decided on their course of action, they rush forward like horses with blinders, looking neither to the right nor left. An obstacle which would frighten discreet men is nothing to determined women. They dare what men avoid, and sometimes they achieve an unusual success.

In Otama's desire to make overtures to Okada, she had delayed so long that a person observing her might have felt impatient because of her indecision. But now that Suezo had told her of his journey to Chiba, she made up her mind to dash toward the port like a ship under full sail in a favorable wind. Suezo, the obstacle in her way, was to remain overnight at Chiba, and the maid was to be at her parents'.

What a delight for Otama to find herself quite free of restraints until the following morning! Since everything had turned out so well for her, she thought that it could only be a good omen that she would attain her object. On that day of all days Okada would most certainly pass her house! Sometimes he came by twice, first in going and then in returning. And even if she missed him once, to do so twice was an impossibility. "I don't care what happens—I'll talk to him today! And once I speak, I'm sure he'll stop to talk," she told herself.

She was a degraded woman, true, a usurer's mistress. But she was even more beautiful than when she had been a virgin. In addition, misfortune had taught her what she wouldn't otherwise have known: somehow men were interested in her. And if this were the case, Okada could not look on her with absolute disfavor. No, that was out of the question. If he had disliked her, he would not have continued to bow to her whenever they saw each other. It was because of this same interest that he had killed the snake for her some time ago. She doubted that he would have offered his assistance if the event had happened at any other house. If it had not happened at her house, he wouldn't even have turned his eyes. Moreover, since she cared for him so much, at least some of her affection, if not all of it, must have been felt by him. "Why, even the birth of a child isn't as difficult as one thinks beforehand," she assured herself.

As she probed her thoughts, she was not aware that the water in the bucket had grown cold.

After she had put away the trays on the shelf, she sat down at her usual place before the charcoal brazier. She felt restless. She took up the pair of tongs and stirred the ashes that Ume had sifted smooth. Then she got up to change into her kimono.

"I'll go to the hairdresser's," she decided.

A good-natured woman who came to Otama to arrange her hair had recommended this shop for special occasions. But up to that time Otama had never gone there.

CHAPTER TWENTY-TWO

narrative shift

IN A EUROPEAN book of children's stories, there is a tale about a peg. I can't remember it well, but it was about a farmer's son who got into a series of difficulties on his journey because the peg in his cartwheel kept coming out. In the story I'm telling now, a mackerel boiled in bean paste had the same effect as that peg.

I was barely able to keep from starving because of the meagre dormitory and boardinghouse meals, yet there was one dish that made my flesh creep. No matter how much air there is in the room or how clean the serving tray is, the moment I see this food, I recall the indescribable odors of the dormitory dining room. When I am served boiled fish with cooked seaweed and wheat gluten cakes, I have that hallucination of smell. And if the boiled fish is mackerel made in bean paste, the sensation is at its peak.

This dish, much to my disgust, was once served for supper at the Kamijo. The maid had set my tray down, but seeing me hesitate in lifting up my chopsticks, which I usually didn't do, she said: "Don't you like mackerel?"

"Well, I don't dislike it. When it's broiled, I can eat it with pleasure. But not when it's boiled in bean paste."

"Oh, I'm sorry. The *okamisan* didn't know. Do you want some eggs instead?" she said, preparing to rise.

"Wait a while," I told her. "I'm not hungry yet, so I'll go out for a walk. Make it look all right to the landlady. Don't say I dislike it. I don't want to give her any trouble."

"But I feel so sorry—"

"Oh forget it."

Seeing me stand to put on my *hakama*, the maid took the tray out into the corridor.

"Are you in, Okada?" I said, calling out to my neighbor.

"Do you want anything?" he asked, his voice clear.

"Nothing in particular, but I'm off for a walk. And I'm going to get some sukiyaki at a restaurant on my way back. Come on along."

"All right. There's something I've been wanting to tell you anyway."

I took my cap off the hook and went out of the Kamijo with my friend. I guess it was after four. Neither of us had talked about the direction to take, but we turned right at the lodginghouse gate.

Just as we were about to go down Muenzaka, I nudged Okada, saying: "Look—there she is!"

"Who?" he asked, in spite of knowing whom I meant, for he turned to the left side to glance at the house with the lattice door.

Otama was standing in front of her house. She would have looked beautiful even if she had been ill. But a young, healthy beauty is made even more beautiful by using make-up, and she was just that. I couldn't tell why, but there was a difference from her usual appearance. I thought she was lovelier than ever. And the radiance of her face dazzled me.

I felt she was transformed as she fixed her eyes on Okada. When he took off his cap, I noticed how upset he was, and I saw him unconsciously quicken his step.

Having the liberty of a third party, I looked back several times and saw that she continued to watch Okada.

He went down the slope with his head bent and without relaxing his hurried gait. I followed him in silence. Opposing thoughts tumbled inside me. They arose from the desire to put myself in Okada's place. But the idea sickened me. Denying my wish, I thought to myself that I couldn't be that base—yet I was annoyed at not being able to repress it effectively.

The thought of putting myself in Okada's place was not that I wanted to surrender to the woman's temptations. I had simply felt that I would have been happy if, like Okada, I had been loved by such a beauty. But how would I have behaved then? I would have kept my freedom of choice, but I wouldn't have run as Okada had just done. I would have visited her, talked with her. I would have kept my virginity, but I would have gone so far as to stop at her house, have conversations with her, love her as one loves a sister. I would have helped her. I would have rescued her from the dirty mud. My imagination had gone that far!

We walked on without speaking until we came to the crossing at the bottom of the slope. After we had passed the police box, I was finally able to talk to Okada.

"Look here," I said, "the situation's getting dangerous."

"What? What's getting dangerous?"

"Don't pretend with me. Why, you must have been thinking about that woman ever since you saw her. I turned around a number of times, and she was always watching you. She's probably standing there right now and looking in this direction. It's just as it's described in the *Saden:* 'His eyes received her and saw her off.' Only in your case it's just the reverse."

"That's enough about her! Since you're the only person I confided in about how I got to know her, you shouldn't tease me."

We reached the edge of the pond and stopped for a moment.

"Should we go that way?" Okada asked, pointing to the northern end of the pond.

I agreed and turned to the left. About ten steps later, I looked at the two-storied houses on the side of the street and said as though talking to myself: "Those houses belong to Fukuchi and Suezo."

"They're a fine contrast. Though I hear the journalist hasn't much integrity either."

"He's a politician too, and a politician," I said without giving much thought to the question, "no matter how he may live, is not free from slander." Perhaps I wanted to make the distance between these two men as wide as possible.

As we talked on in this way and crossed a small bridge leading to the north end of the pond, we saw a young man in student uniform standing at the water's edge and watching something. At our approach he shouted: "Hello there."

It was Ishihara, a student who was interested in jujitsu and who read only those books related to his major subject. Neither Okada nor I knew him well, but we didn't dislike him.

"What are you looking at around here?" I asked.

Without answering he pointed across the water. We stared in that direction through the gray vagueness of the evening air. In those days, rushes grew all over the section of the pond from the Nezu ditch to where we were now standing. The withered stalks became more and more sparse toward the center of the pond, where only dried up lotus leaves like bunches of rags and seed sacs like sponges were seen here and there with stems broken at various heights into acute angles. They lent a picturesque desolation to the scene. Among these bitumen-colored stems and over the dark gray surface of the water reflecting faint lights, we saw a dozen wild geese slowly moving back and forth. Some rested motionless on the water.

"Can you throw that far with a stone?" Ishihara asked, turning to Okada.

"Of course, but I don't know if I can hit anything or not."

"Go ahead. Try."

Okada hesitated. "They're going to sleep, aren't they? It's cruel to throw at them."

Ishihara laughed. "Don't be sentimental! If you don't, then I will."

"Then I'll make them fly away," said Okada, reluctantly picking up a stone.

The small stone hissed faintly through the air. I watched where it landed, and I saw the neck of a goose drop down. At the same time a few flapped their wings and, uttering cries, dispersed and glided over the water. But they did not rise high into the air. The one that was hit remained where it was.

"Excellent shot!" Ishihara cried. He looked at the surface of the water for a short time and said: "I'll get it. But help me a little."

"How can you?" Okada asked. Like him, I was eager to hear the answer.

"Now's not a good time," said Ishihara. "In half an hour it'll be dark. And then I can easily get it. I won't need your help in actually going out there, but be here then and do what I tell you. And then I'll treat you to a feast!"

"It sounds all right," said Okada. "But what will you do until then?"

"I'll wander around here. You two go wherever you wish. If all three of us stay, it'll attract attention."

"Then let's go once around the pond," I suggested to Okada.

He agreed, and we started out.

CHAPTER TWENTY-THREE

OKADA and I crossed the end of Hanazono-cho and went toward the stone steps leading to the Toshogu Shrine. For some time we walked in silence.

"Poor bird," said Okada, as if speaking to himself.

Without any logical connection the woman of Muen-zaka came into my mind.

"You see," Okada said, this time to me, "I only meant to throw in their direction."

"I know," I said, still thinking of the woman.

After some time I added: "But it'll be interesting to see how Ishihara intends to get the bird."

"Yes," said Okada, walking on and thinking of something. Perhaps the wild goose occupied his thoughts.

As we turned south at the foot of the stone steps, we went on towards the Benten Shrine, but the death of the bird had depressed us and had broken our talk into fragments.

Passing before the entrance of the shrine, Okada suddenly said: "I almost forgot what I wanted to tell you." It seemed as though it were an effort for him to turn his thoughts in another direction.

His news startled me. He had planned to tell me in my room that night, but he had gone out at my invitation.

And then it had occurred to him to reveal it at the restaurant, but since that now seemed unlikely, he had decided to explain it during our walk. It was this.

"I'm going abroad before graduation. I've already got my passport from the Foreign Ministry. And I've sent in the notice that I'm giving up graduating. You know the German professor who's been studying endemic diseases in the Orient. Well, he employed me under the arrangement that he would give me four thousand marks for the trip to Germany and back, along with two hundred marks each month. He was looking for a student who could read Chinese and also speak German. Professor Baelz had recommended me, so I went and took the examination. I had to translate several passages from classical Chinese medical books into German, but I passed. And I got the contract right then."

The Leipzig University professor would take Okada and help him pass his doctoral examinations. Okada had received permission to use as his graduation thesis the medical literature of the Orient to be translated by him for the doctor.

"I'm moving from the Kamijo tomorrow to the doctor's house at Tsukiji. I'll pack the books he's collected in China and Japan. Then I'll help him on a research project in Kyushu. And from there we take a Messageries Maritimes ship."

I paused often in our walk to say how surprised I was and to praise Okada's determination, but I was under the impression that we had gone very slowly as we spoke. Yet when he finished, I looked at my watch and found that only ten minutes had passed since we left Ishihara. And we had already walked two-thirds of the way around the pond and were coming to the end of Ike-no-hata Street.

"It's too soon to go on ahead," I said.

"Let's have a bowl of noodles," Okada suggested.

"All right," I said at once, and we retraced our steps to the restaurant.

While eating, Okada said: "It's too bad I have to give up graduation when I'm so near to it. But if I missed this chance, I'd never be able to go to Europe. I doubt if I could ever get abroad at government expense."

"Well, it's too good an opportunity to miss. Who cares about graduating? If you get a doctor's certificate in Europe, it's certainly no disadvantage. And even if you don't, it won't matter much."

"That's what I've been thinking. Going abroad will give me better qualifications—it's my one concession to the way of the world."

"Are you ready to go? I suppose you've been quite busy with preparations."

"No, I'm going in these clothes. The doctor told me that Western suits made by Japanese tailors won't do in Europe."

"I can imagine. I once remember reading that the editor of the *Kagetsu Shinshi* went aboard at Yokohama with no preparations at all."

"I read that article too. According to it, he didn't even let his family know he was leaving. But I wrote a long letter to my parents."

"How I envy you! You'll have the professor, and you'll never feel inconvenienced on your trip. I can't even imagine what it will be like."

"Neither can I. But yesterday I did visit Professor Shokei Shibata. He's taken an interest in me. And when I told him, he gave me a guidebook he had written."

"Oh? I didn't know he'd even written one."

"He wrote it all right, but it's not for sale. He told me he had it printed to give to country bumpkins!"

As we talked on in this way, I suddenly realized that we had only five minutes before our appointment. We hurried out of the restaurant and went to meet Ishihara, who was waiting for us. The pond was in darkness, and only the Benten Shrine's red color was visible in the gathering haze.

Ishihara, who had been looking for us, brought us to the edge of the water and said: "It's all right now. All the other geese have shifted their positions. I'll start now. You two stand here and give me directions. Look. About six yards from here you see a broken lotus stem falling to the right. Now in line with that is another stem lower than that one and falling to the left. I have to make my way along that line. Now, if you see me get off even a bit, shout out to me either 'right' or 'left' and put me straight."

"We understand," said Okada. "We've studied the principle of parallax! But isn't the water too deep for you?"

"Not enough to go over my head," Ishihara said, taking off his clothes.

When he stepped into the pond, the muddy water was just above his knees. Raising one leg at a time and planting each alternately, he plodded on like a heron. The water was deeper in certain areas than in others.

Soon Ishihara passed the two stems of lotus, and presently Okada directed him to the right, whereupon Ishihara went a little in that direction. "Left!" Okada shouted next, for Ishihara had gone too far over.

Suddenly Ishihara stopped short, stooped, and at once began to retrace his steps. And by the time he had passed the farther lotus stem, we could see the game hanging from his right hand.

He reached the edge of the water, the mud staining his legs only to the middle of his thighs. The prize was an uncommonly large bird. After Ishihara had washed carelessly, he dressed quickly. Few passersby ever came to this section of the pond, and no one had appeared during the time Ishihara was in the water and had come back.

"How should we carry it?" I asked.

Putting on his *hakama*, Ishihara said: "How about Okada's putting it under his cloak? It's bigger than ours. And I'll have the bird cooked at my lodging!"

He lived in a rented room of a private family. Apparently his landlady's only virtue was her wickedness, and we could stop her from telling what we had done by giving her a piece of the goose. The house was somewhere in the back part of a winding alley.

Ishihara briefly explained the course we would take. We could approach his house from two ways. One route lay south through Kiridoshi, the other north through Muenzaka. These two directions formed a circle around the Iwasaki mansion. There was little difference in the distance between them. But that wasn't the present question. It was the police box, and there was one each way.

We weighed the advantages and disadvantages, and we concluded that we had better not take the more frequented way through Kiridoshi but the less traveled one through Muenzaka. The best procedure was for Okada to carry the goose under his cloak and for the two of us to flank him and make him look less conspicuous.

Okada seemed resigned; he smiled and took the bird. But in whatever way he carried it, the tail feathers emerged a few inches from the edge of his cloak. In addition, the lower part of Okada's cloak was expanded in a curious way so that he looked like a circular cone.

It was up to Ishihara and me to make Okada appear as natural as possible.

CHAPTER TWENTY-FOUR

"ALL RIGHT," Ishihara said, "let's start." And we set out with Okada between us. From the first, our concern had

116

been the police box at the crossing below Muenzaka. So Ishihara lectured us on our mental attitude in passing the box in question. It was, to sum up what I heard, that we should not waver in our equilibrium of mind; that if we wavered, there would be a gap; and that if there were a gap, it would give the antagonist the advantage.

"The tiger doesn't eat a drunken man," Ishihara said, quoting an old Chinese proverb.

It seemed to me that his speech was nothing more than what his jujitsu master had told him.

"Do you mean then," said Okada playfully, "that a policeman's a tiger and we are drunks?"

"*Silentium!*" exclaimed Ishihara.

We were approaching the corner to go to Muenzaka. As we turned up the slope, we saw a policeman standing at the crossing.

Ishihara, who was close to Okada's left side, said suddenly: "Do you know the formula for calculating the volume of a cone? What? You don't! It's simple. Since volume is one-third the area of the base times the height, if the base is a circle, you can get it by one-third of the radius squared times pi times the height. And if you remember that pi equals 3.1416, it's the simplest of problems. I know the value of pi up to the eighth decimal. 3.14159265! For all practical purposes, the figures after that are unnecessary."

During this speech we passed the crossing. The policeman was in front of his station on the left side of the narrow street we were coming along; stationed there, he was watching a rickshaw running from Kaya-cho towards Nezu. He looked at us for only a moment.

"Why," I asked Ishihara, "did you start calculating the volume of a cone?"

But at the same time I recognized a woman in the middle of the slope looking toward us. My heart felt a strange shock. All the way from the northern end of the

pond I had been thinking about her instead of the policeman at his box. I didn't know why, but I imagined she
would be waiting for Okada. And I hadn't been wrong.
She had come down the slope about two or three houses
from her own.

I was careful not to attract Ishihara's attention, and
I looked quickly at the woman and Okada, from one to
the other. His delicate coloring was a shade deeper. He
brushed the vizor of his cap, pretending to set it right.
The woman's face seemed as hard as stone. But her eyes,
opened beautifully wide, seemed to contain an infinite
wistfulness of parting.

Ishihara's answer to my question was mere sound in
my ears. He had probably said that he thought of the
formula because of the shape of Okada's cloak.

Ishihara had also noticed the woman, but his only
comment was "There's a beauty!" And then he continued his speech, adding: "I taught you the secret of
the mind's equilibrium. You've not had any training in
it, and I was afraid you couldn't carry off our scheme
at the critical moment. So I devised a plan to shift your
attention. Anything might have done, but I thought of
the cone as I just explained it. At any rate, my technique
has met with success! Thanks to the formula of a cone,
you were able to get beyond the policeman and maintain
an *unbefangen* attitude!"

The three of us came to a portion of the road turning
east along the Iwasaki mansion. In an alley that was not
wide enough to accommodate two rickshaws, we were in
little danger of being seen. Ishihara left Okada's side and
marched before us like a leader.

I looked back once more, but the woman was no longer
in sight.

We stayed at Ishihara's until late that night. It might
be said that we were forced to keep Ishihara company

while he drank a great deal of saké and ate the flesh of the goose. And since Okada said nothing about his trip abroad, I had to hold back my desire to discuss it at length. Instead, I was forced to listen to their personal experiences in the regatta.

When we returned to the Kamijo, I went to bed at once. I was drunk and tired, so I couldn't talk to Okada. And when I came back from the university the next day, I found that he had already gone.

Just as great events happen because of a peg, a dish of boiled mackerel at a Kamijo supper prevented Otama and Okada from ever meeting each other. This is not all of that story. But the events beyond it are outside the present narrative.

Now that I have written this, I have counted on my fingers and discovered that thirty-five years have passed since then. I learned half the story during my close association with Okada. And I learned the other half from Otama, with whom I accidentally became acquainted after Okada had left the country.

In the same way that one receives an image through a stereoscope, the two pictures set together under the lens, I created this story by comparing and combining what I knew earlier and what I heard later. *time wasn't linear*

Some of my readers may ask: "How did you get to know Otama? And when did you hear the story from her?"

But as I said before, the answers to those questions are beyond the scope of my story. It is unnecessary to say that I lack the requisites that would qualify me to be Otama's lover; still, let me warn my readers that it is best not to indulge in fruitless speculation.

Not how I expected the story to end.

Other TUT BOOKS available:

Please order from your bookstore or write directly to:

CHARLES E. TUTTLE CO., INC.
Suido 1-chome, 2–6, Bunkyo-ku, Tokyo 112
or: Rutland, Vermont 05701 U.S.A.